# Rick Amato
# A Pocket Full of Pennies

# Rick Amato
# A Pocket Full of Pennies

THOMAS NELSON PUBLISHERS®
Nashville

A Division of Thomas Nelson, Inc.
www.ThomasNelson.com

Published in Nashville, Tennessee, by Thomas Nelson, Inc.

Library of Congress Cataloging-in-Publication Data:
94-068469

4  5  6  7  8  9  PHX  05  04  03  02  01

In loving memory of Denise Amato.
Her struggle against cancer
has inspired us all to new heights
of greatness.

## Dedication

I dedicate this book, my first, to Yeshua, the carpenter from Nazareth. He dared to become a Son of Man that I might dare to become a Son of God.
Rick Amato
Detroit, August 1994

## Acknowledgment

No words are adequate to thank my family. My precious wife Nancy Jean and our five children—Beth Anne, Nancy Jean, Joseph Richard, Sara Elizabeth, and Mary Grace. I also praise God for my daughter Beth's husband, Matt Thisse, one of my Timothy's in the faith. They keep my inner fire burning brightly.

A special thanks to all of my partners and my loving and devoted staff. They keep me from burning out.

Finally, deep gratitude is expressed to Ted Squires and the Ministry Services Division of Thomas Nelson, Inc. Where I saw ashes, they saw a phoenix.

# Contents

# What's so Important About a Penny?

As this fourth printing of *A Pocketful of Pennies* takes place, I can honestly say that I feel I've been part of the beginning of a great spiritual awakening worldwide. I can also tell you that there are many people calling for the abolition of the American penny as a use in our currency. Some people might wonder what these things have in common. More specifically, what's so important about a penny anyways?

Not too many steps from where I am sitting here in my home in Woodhaven, Michigan, there is a very old container that was handed down to my Grandfather, John D. Miller, from his Mother, to my Mother, Betty Jo (Miller) Amato, and then down to me. Inside this glass container are more than 400 pennies. I have it put up in a special place where I can see it regularly.

These 400 pennies are only the pennies that I have saved in a little over a year's time. Pennies found, not only throughout the United States, but also in different parts of the world. I can't explain it. I also can't deny it. I have found *a lot* of pennies since I first wrote this book.

My mind goes back today to the time that I interviewed President Mikhail Gorbachev, the final president of the former Soviet Union, for television. The president said for me to go downstairs, take my shoes off, put my feet up, and someone would bring me a glass of lemonade. I was so surprised to find a United States of America penny on President Gorbachev's footrest in Moscow, Russia.

I also think of the time that the great NFL, future Hall of Fame football player and man of God, Reggie White, took his family, along with many of his supporters and some of my family and I to Greece. We were stopped for a brief time in Ankara, Turkey when we stepped up to a counter to buy a Coca-Cola. When I looked down in the sand, next to my foot was, you guessed it, an American penny!

The simple point I'm trying to make is that I really find pennies all over the world with a consistency that amazes my friends and loved ones. Many of them, like me, have also begun picking up pennies, believing them to be a sign that God has gone on the path before them. I am convinced that someone travels ahead of me and puts pennies down on the ground wherever I go, precisely in the steps of my path to let me know that someone much bigger and smarter than me has gone before me, and as the great Psalmist David prayed, "You know the path that I take . . . my steps are ordered by you" (Psalm 35).

I find myself grasping for words when I try to describe the events that my eyes have seen. I cannot explain to you the synchronicity with which things have happened in my life. Whenever I needed to talk to someone, it seemed like they appeared. Whenever there was a certain thing that I needed to do in order to fulfill what I thought was God's will for my life, the preaching of the Cross in all of the world, it would be made possible to happen.

The major point of *A Pocketful of Pennies* is simple. It's a spiritual truth that many people on earth are beginning to embrace. It's also a fact that even modern science, with amazing advances in the neurosciences as well as quantum Physics, is beginning to explore. The simple fact is: *there are no coincidences*.

The fact of the matter is that every human on earth can know God, including you. Every single person can see miracles. You don't have to be a Moses or a Jesus or a Buddha to have a profound spiritual experience. You only need to find a penny.

In spiritual terms that means that you only need to be aware of the miracles that happen around you everyday, like when you want to talk to somebody and you pick up the phone and they're there. Or, when you need something only to be diverted from searching for it to run into something else you needed which was really more important. This is called synchronicity.

When I first wrote *A Pocketful of Pennies*, I never dreamed that so many people would write me to tell me that they too have a large penny collection now, and they all tell me that, like me, the pennies they find are in significant times in their life, just when they need to find them the most. It seems that whoever or whatever drops these pennies in our path seems to know when we most need to find them.

Now there are some people who would call this superstition or some sort of mystical poppycock or New Age hocus-pocus. No, not really, they're just pennies. Bright shiny ones, dull ones, chipped ones, and new ones. Just pennies.

Pennies scattered along the path of life for those of us who dare to believe something bigger than us is happening that makes us all a part of a whole. Something that helps us to believe that we are more than the collective functioning of myriads of neurotransmitters and more than a mass of electrochemical energy. Proof that we are all fragmented, yet functioning parts, of a whole, working together with a purpose.

Just pennies that remind us that, "All things are working together for the good of those who love God" (Romans 8:28). Little miracles along the way, but *miracles* nonetheless.

No one will ever convince me that it wasn't God or one of His very large staff who scattered them at precisely the right moments and precisely the right places so that I would know that the One who walks *with* me has also gone *before* me. I know there is a God. I know miracles still happen, because I have a pocket full of pennies.

I hope after reading this book you quickly begin gathering pennies for your own special glass jar, whether it's a tin can that you just found or something passed down from generation to generation. Pick up every single one you find. Take note of where you found them. God is everywhere, but only those who will stop and acknowledge Him become aware of His awesome presence and the ability He has to turn the darkest nightmares of our life into beautiful dreams. He does this, not through some huge miracle or some great grand display of His magnificent power, but through the little miracles and events that happen on a daily basis, and teach us to be like Jesus. As we come to know Him to be eternal spirit may His name be praised forever.

So here's praying that this book does for you what it did for me and so many tens of thousands of others. Here's praying that the God who loves you more than you could ever imagine, in ways you could never dream of, will begin to show Himself to you today in the smallest minutia of your life. Here's hoping that you'll begin discovering the daily miracles in your own life. I call them pennies, and I have a pocket full of them. Here's hoping that soon you will too.

Your Fellow Penny Picker Upper

Dr. Rick Amato
Woodhaven, Michigan
August, 2001

# A Pocket Full of Pennies

## Preface

I, Rick Amato, grandson of an Italian immigrant, husband, father, and preacher of the Gospel of the Lord Jesus Christ, have a pocket full of pennies. I find them everywhere I go. No matter what I'm doing, I seem to find pennies—and sometimes in the most unexpected places. Not everyone who sees pennies picks them up, but I do. I pocket each and every one I see, bright and shiny or dull and worn, because they're reminders to me of the overwhelming grace of God and of His power and presence in my life. Over the years I've collected more pennies than I can count.

You see, I am a Christian—a follower of Jesus Christ—and the goal of my life is simply to know God and to make Him known. I want to know Him, like the apostle Paul said, *"and the power of His resurrection and the fellowship of His sufferings, being conformed to His death; in order that I may attain to the resurrection from the dead"* (Phil. 3:10-11, *NASB*).

I'm convinced the reason many of us never get to know God in His fullness is that we're constantly expecting Him to manifest Himself in some fantastic, parting-the-Red Sea kind of way. We're expecting healing from physical disease, impressive material provisions—the stuff of genuine, verifiable, modern-day miracles. God certainly can, and sometimes still does, bless us in these spectacular ways. But more often, in fact daily, He is at work in our lives, bringing about miraculous changes in you and me through "ordinary" means. Pennies.

God gives us "spiritual pennies"—lots of them—from His storehouse of love. He scatters a few around for us each and every day. If we're looking for them, we'll find them—and when we do, if we are wise, we'll pick them up. Even if they look worthless. Even if they're dull or tarnished. Even if bending over for them seems like too much trouble. Because in God's paradoxical economy, they're priceless treasures.

My spiritual journey has not been a smooth one, but I can tell you this: God has never stopped loving me. I have hurt others, hurt myself, and hurt the kingdom of God. But He has never stopped blessing me or using me. And I have found that some of my darkest days were miraculous pennies in His hands. God's Word says it like this:

> For consider your calling, brethren, that there were not many wise according to the flesh, not many mighty, not many noble; but God has chosen the foolish things of the world to shame the wise, and God has chosen the weak things of the world to shame the things which are strong, and the base things of the world and the despised, God has chosen, the things that are not, that He might nullify the things that are, that no man should boast before God. But by His doing you are in Christ Jesus, who became to us wisdom from God, and righteousness and sanctification, and redemption, that, just as it is written, "LET HIM WHO BOASTS, BOAST IN THE LORD" (1 Cor. 1:26-31, NASB).

There isn't much I can boast of, as the pages of this book will reveal . . . but I know God. And if you'll walk with me through these pages, you will too. I am not rich, or wise, or powerful, but He has used me to speak His name to millions, from the down-and-out addicts in the streets to the rulers of nations in seats of power.

Watching for miracles like those performed in the Bible—healing the blind or raising the dead or feeding a multitude with a sack lunch—is like looking for bags containing lots of crisp, new dollar bills. Your search won't pay off very often. Maybe never. But God's little miracles—His pennies—are all over the place. In the words of British poet Elizabeth Barrett Browning: "Earth's crammed with heaven, and every common bush afire with God; but only he who sees takes off his shoes."

I'm convinced that if you stop and look, you'll see what I've come to see: that God shows Himself consistently in the commonplace—and that He can teach us great truths from what might seem insignificant or unwanted at first glance. These are a few of the pennies God has brought my way and what I have learned from them. My prayer is that they will teach you as well, and maybe even inspire you to become a "penny collector" too.

Rick Amato
Detroit, Michigan
July, 1994

# No Other Name
## The Penny of Salvation

*It is only when you ask a question out of your
very bowels that the answer is really an answer. It is
only when you stretch out your hands for it until
your arms ache that the gift is really a gift.*
—Frederick Buechner

In 1974, I was a rebellious kid. My teenage years coincided with the drug-happy early seventies, and I participated fully. Like a lot of young people, I was searching. Who was I, really? Where did I come from? Why was I here? What was life all about? Was it all over when you died? The close-knit family of my childhood was little more than a fuzzy memory since, by the time I entered high school, both my parents were chasing hard after the "American dream." Dad went to work every morning at 5:00 and came home at 3:00 in the afternoon to change clothes and head off to a second job. Mom went back to work to pay for a second car, and soon she was working two jobs as well. My three brothers and three sisters were growing up and going off in different directions. But I wanted the stability of a solid family—so I found my own.

The kids waiting in the back alley of our Detroit, Michigan, home were more than happy to be my surrogate family. We hung out together, smoked cigarettes, and tried to be cool. One day a friend from the alley handed me a different kind of cigarette—a joint. I smoked it, and it felt pretty good. I figured if one felt good, two would feel better. And you know what? I was right. Then I started mixing pot and pills to get the same high. Before long, drug use was a daily, desperate habit, not just something to do on Friday or Saturday nights for kicks. I started out just playing around with getting high, but I ended up hooked. Substance abuse became a way of life.

## An Unusual Invitation

One night my buddies and I were out drinking and smoking dope, and one of them, Marty Hall, came out with what had to be the silliest question any of us had ever heard.

"Who's going to church with me tomorrow morning?" he asked.

"Say what?" I couldn't believe what I was hearing.

He repeated the question. "Who will go to church with me? My dad's making me go to church tomorrow, and I don't want to go by myself. Come on and go with me, okay?"

"No way!" we all responded.

"How about you, Rick?" Marty asked.

"Uh-uh, no way. Not me." I answered.

Then he sweetened the offer a little. "We could smoke a couple of joints of Colombian and go catch a grin off the preacher. What do you say?"

Now he was talking! "What time are you picking me up?" I asked.

On Sunday morning I got up and picked my Afro out high and wide and dressed for the occasion: black pants, black sweater, black crushed velvet blazer, black socks, and fluorescent orange platform boots. If I was going to church, I was going to go in style. Marty came for me at the appointed time, and I can't speak for him, but I marched into that little Baptist church a defiant dude. I had no intention of listening or learning. I had no plans to hear or respond to anything. I was there to mock the preacher, the service, and the people gathered there. I just wanted to check it all out for laughs. But something happened that day that changed my life.

## An Unforgettable Message of Love

The preacher stood up, and I didn't plan to, but I began to listen. "Christianity," he said, "isn't about rules and regulations. It isn't about do's and don'ts. It isn't about Catholics, Methodists, Baptists, Charismatics, Episcopalians or Lutherans. Christianity is about a man named Jesus Christ. He was the only man who ever lived who never told a lie, never stole anything, and never had an evil thought in his life.

"Christianity is the story of how God loves you so much that He gave His one and only Son—that man Jesus who had never done anything wrong—for you. Jesus hung on the cross wounded and dying, and every time His heart beat, the blood of the only Son of God flowed down into the dirt of Golgotha. His hands and feet were pierced. His side was ripped open.

"When Jesus was on the cross," the pastor went on, "He never questioned why he was there. He never said, 'Why the nails, God? Why the spear?' Instead, He said 'My God, My God, why have You left me alone?' And the reason His Father God had left Him alone was because He was taking someone's place there. Yours. He was carrying your sin. He had chosen to die in disgrace so you wouldn't have to."

Although I didn't know it, I came to that little Baptist church as a young man who was searching: for meaning in life, for someone to love me for who I was, for friends, for acceptance. And for something I hadn't thought much about before—for forgiveness. That day, in Marty Hall's church, I understood that Jesus died for me because I was lost. I still didn't know where I'd come from or what I was here for, and I certainly didn't know where I was going when I died, but when the preacher reached the part in his story where he said, "On the third day, Jesus Christ rose from the dead," I suddenly realized this wasn't some storybook tale. This might be real, and I might believe it.

## Just As I Am

While all these thoughts were racing in my mind, the congregation stood and began to sing an old, familiar hymn, "Just As I Am." When I heard the words "Just as I am, without one plea—but that Thy blood was shed for me," I felt that God really did love me. And I knew that I needed to let this Jesus who died for me into my heart. I longed to step out and move toward the altar, to ask Him to be my Lord and the Savior I so desperately needed, but as the song continued, my enthusiasm began to waver. I was having second thoughts. "No," I told myself. "This is crazy. I've never even believed in God."

As I held onto the pew thinking *I can't do it—no way*, I heard the words to the first verse again: "Just as I am, without one plea . . ." Again I fought with myself. This is emotionalism. These people are not normal. It's only the music that is making you feel this way. At that very moment the preacher turned and seemed to look right at me. "You may be here this morning, and you think it is the music that's calling you to be saved. Well it's not. It's the spirit of Jesus."

That did it. Without another moment's hesitation, I leaned over to my friend and said, "Excuse me, Marty. I'm going down front." I knelt down at the altar, and I don't know that I had all the theological information straight in my mind, but whatever I did have was enough. On my knees, I said these words: "Lord, Jesus Christ, come into my heart. If You're there, I want to be saved. I don't want to go to hell. Come live inside me right now." It was the beginning of a new life.

## All Seekers Welcome

Through my searching, God showed the penny of salvation. The good news is that He still welcomes seekers today—and better yet, He wants to be found. The God of the Bible is a God who opens His arms wide to the man or woman searching for meaning and purpose in life. For a friend. For love. For forgiveness.

Searching can be a painful process. It can be frightening and achingly lonely. But there is an end to our searching that far outweighs its pain. Jeremiah 29:11–13 reveals it:

> *"For I know the plans that I have for you," declares the* LORD, *"plans for welfare and not for calamity to give you a future and a hope. Then you will call upon Me and come and pray to Me, and I will listen to you. And you will seek Me and find Me, when you search for Me with all your heart"* (NASB).

For a real-life example of how God welcomes the seeker, you can't beat the Bible's account of the prodigal son. In it, a young man seeking satisfaction, identity, and freedom left home with an early inheritance to find his own way. (His older, less adventurous brother stayed home.) Far, far from home, the young man tasted all that the world had to offer (and that his inherited money could buy). Since there's always more world to be had than money to pay for it, he finally spent all that he had. He was broke—and his timing could not have been worse. A famine occurred in the far country where he had wandered, and he experienced real need, perhaps for the first time in his life.

Part-time employment was the best he could do for himself, and the job he found was less than glamorous. He fed pigs. When he became so hungry that the pigs' food began to look good to him, he came to his senses.

"My father's hired hands have bread to eat," he thought, "and here I am dying of hunger." So he hatched a plan. He would go home, present himself as a failure, confess his sin, and beg to be put on his father's payroll, certain that he no longer deserved to be received as a son. And that is just what he did. Only, it didn't work out the way he imagined it would.

When his father saw the younger son coming—while he was still a long way off, the Bible says—he saw him, felt compassion for him, and ran to him. Kissed him. Embraced him. Cut off his planned speech mid-sentence. Announced plans for a homecoming celebration the likes of which no one had ever seen and said these words about his boy who had searched and come up empty: *"Quickly, bring out the best robe and put it on him, and put a ring on his hand and sandals on his feet; and bring the fattened calf, kill it, and let us eat and be merry; for this son of mine was dead, and has come to life again; he was lost, and has been found"* (Luke 15:22–24, NASB).

The prodigal son searched long and hard for satisfaction, and spent all that he had in the process. In the end, he came up empty, and you and I do too, unless we realize that God is the ultimate object of our search. Jesus said, *"Blessed are those who hunger and thirst for righteousness, for they shall be satisfied"* (Matt. 5:6, NASB). God ran to meet the prodigal, and He ran to meet me. The end was worth the search.

## A New Reason for Living

God did for me exactly what I asked Him to. He saved me. My illegal drug use began to cease that day. My habits began to change. Now instead of getting high with my friends after school, I would run home every day from football, baseball, or wrestling practice, go into my bedroom, and read. I would read the book of Matthew, then I would pray. I'd read the book of Luke and pray. I'd read the book of John, and then I'd pray. My parents thought

I'd really gone over the edge this time—over God. They even called the preacher and said, "Our son has lost his mind. He's gone from doing drugs to being a religious fanatic."

The preacher and others tried to reassure them. "He'll get over it," they said. But I didn't. I never have. When you've sought long and hard for something and you find it, the thrill doesn't just go away. I had looked for a reason for living, and I found it.

My preaching career began soon after God saved me. One day I tossed my Bible on top of the cleats in my gym bag and headed off for school. At football practice that afternoon, the coach would say "God ___," and I would say "Praise God!" Every time he'd say "Jesus Christ!" I'd say, "is Lord."

My first "sermon" was preached to the high school choir. All the kids were gathered together in the choir room, waiting for the presidential address. And I was the president. I got up and said, "This year's presidential address is found in John, chapter 3, verse 7. Jesus said, 'You must be born again.'"

One guy yelled, "Hey, man. This is public school. You can't preach the Bible in public school."

I said, "Shut up! I'm the choir president, and this is the presidential address. I can do whatever I want." And I did. I told them that when I received Jesus, all my sins were forgiven. That I was clean for the first time in my life. That I knew I was going to heaven. I told them how wonderful it was. Then the bell rang and I lost my congregation. All except for the biggest, baddest, strongest dude in the whole school. His name was Norman "The Tower of Power" Maurer. But we just called him Igor.

He looked at me. I looked at him.

"Hey, Amato," he said.

"Me?" I asked.

"Yeah, you. Come here."

Hesitantly, I walked over to Norman, wondering just what he was going to do to me. He said, "Do you really believe that if a person asks Jesus Christ into his life that He'll forgive everything that person ever did?"

"Yes," I squeaked.

"You mean He will save him?" Norman asked.

"Yes, yes," I stuttered. "That's right."

Then he quietly said, "Save me."

"What?"

"Save me," he repeated. "Right now."

Nothing in my short preaching career had prepared me for this.

"I don't know how."

Norman yelled at me. "Why are you telling people to get saved if you don't know how to save them?"

"We didn't get to that part yet," I told him.

"Well," he asked, "what did you do?"

I thought for a minute. "I got down on my knees."

Norman got down on his knees.

I was gaining confidence. "Now, you dirty, rotten, wicked sinner, tell God that you believe Jesus died for your sins. Open up your heart and let Him come in."

Then you wouldn't believe what happened. All of a sudden, big tears welled up in Norman's eyes. "Oh God," he said, "I'm sorry. Please, God, save me."

Another searcher found what he was looking for. The school had a new All-American athlete, and Rick Amato had a new bodyguard. Now there were two of us. Norman and I. And what God did in my life and in Norman's, I have seen Him do over and over again in the years since. He began to use us right where we were—on a high school football team. The next day at practice, the coach gave me the ball and told me to cut right. I cut left. "Jesus Christ!" he shouted in frustration.

I said, "is Lord."

Norm said, "is Lord."

The coach looked at Norman and said, "You too, Norm?"

"Yep." Norman nodded.

The coach took his hat off and looked up to heaven. He said, "Jesus Christ, I am sorry for taking Your name in vain in front of these kids, but I'm so frustrated. Our football team is 0–13." After a moment he continued, "Please God. I'll quit taking Your name in vain if You'll teach them how to play football."

Again, God did what He was asked to do. Before every practice, I led our team in a prayer. After practice, Norman led in prayer. But in between, something else began to happen. We learned to play football and we started winning games. The next year, instead of going 0–13, we went 9–3. The year after that, the team went undefeated and went to the state championship. But the most important business took place not on the football field but in the hearts of a bunch of young guys who were searching just like Norman and me. By the time we reached the state finals, many of our teammates had made professions of faith in Jesus Christ. On the way home from the playoffs, Norm told me our bus was rocking with shouts and chants, not of "We're number one," but of "Praise the Lord! Praise the Lord!" We were on a winning team at last.

## It's the Seekers Who Find

Have you ever wondered if God is real? For many of us, that is the unspoken question of our deepest heart. Voicing it may be out of the question, but it sneaks into our thoughts just the same. Is He real? Does He care about me? Is there a divine purpose and plan behind the confusion of my life? It's okay to ask. In fact, the questions themselves are an exercise in honesty. Most people, although they never question God's existence verbally, clearly demonstrate by their actions that they doubt He exists. Even some who go by His name seem to live their daily lives as if their sole ambition were to disprove His reality. But it's the seekers who find.

Saint Augustine said that man's spirit is restless until it finds its rest in God. Each of us—you, me, Norman Maurer—is created with a God-shaped vacuum that only He can fill. In our searching we may try to fill it with other things or other relationships, but they never ultimately satisfy because at its very heart, our longing is a "God-longing." No matter how many counselors we talk to, no matter how many self-help books we read, no matter how many seminars we attend or how much success we attain, we will continue to search until we find the only thing that satisfies our God-longing. And that is God Himself.

## Getting to Know God

For Norman and me and for the rest of the guys whose lives were changed that year, the journey was just beginning. The searching had led us to the penny of salvation, but there was so much more to know of God than just His power to save. You see, we were not instantly *perfected*, just instantly *forgiven*. Why didn't we become perfect when we were forgiven? Because getting to know God involves a lifetime of learned behavior and developed disciplines. Knowing God starts with faith, but it doesn't end there. As Paul wrote to the believers at Colossae,

> As you therefore have received Christ Jesus the Lord, so walk in Him, having been firmly rooted and now being built up in Him and established in your faith, just as you were instructed, and overflowing with gratitude. See to it that no one takes you captive through philosophy and empty deception, according to the tradition of men, according to the elementary principles of the world, rather than according to Christ (Col. 2:6–8, NASB).

God is a rewarder of those who diligently seek Him, but once we've taken that first step of faith, we need to keep walking. To become aware of His actions and activities in our lives. To strive to know Him. The benefits that are ours through this process called *sanctification* are tremendous. As we come to know Him, He transforms our pain into power. He turns our weaknesses into strengths. He makes our mistakes into miracles. Our tragedies become God's triumphs.

We start by acknowledging God's existence. Then we must receive His Son Jesus into our hearts by faith. The same sinner's prayer that Norman and I said as teenagers is the prayer that every man or woman who would know God must eventually offer up. It's the prayer of faith in Christ that "cleans the slate" and puts the Spirit of the living God within us. Our enemy, Satan, would rather hear us say anything than words of surrender to Jesus Christ. He knows that once we believe in Christ and receive Him "by grace through faith," he has lost all power over us.

In Christ, there is new meaning and purpose for life. In Christ, there is real worth. In Christ, we no longer need the approval of others to feel good about who and what we are, and we are set free from the performance trap that says identity comes from doing. In Christ, you and I don't have to "measure up" to know love and acceptance.

Because of His sacrifice, we can accept ourselves, based not on our performance but on His completed action on our behalf. On the cross, Jesus deemed Rick Amato worth dying for. My search for love can cease when I grasp the unconditional, undeserved, unending love of God made evident through the death of His Son. And how do you know that God loves you? Because Christ died for you, too.

> For while we were still helpless, at the right time Christ died for the ungodly. For one will hardly die for a righteous man; though perhaps for the good man someone would dare even to die. But God demonstrates His own love toward us, in that while

*we were yet sinners, Christ died for us (Rom. 5:6-8, NASB).*

My greatest hope for you is that you find the Lord Jesus Christ through your searching and that you will come to know, as the apostle Peter did many years ago, that nothing else will satisfy your heart.

"You do not want to go away also, do you?" Jesus asked Simon Peter after some of his followers had deserted Him.

"Lord, to whom shall we go?" he responded. "You have words of eternal life. And we have believed and have come to know that You are the Holy One of God."

There is salvation in no other name. Wherever your searching began, let it end in Him.

## A Prayer for Salvation

*Lord Jesus, they say Your name in the Hebrew language is* Yashua, *which means salvation. I praise that name.*

*I've looked for satisfaction, peace, and purpose for so long. I've looked for them in worldly achievements, worldly relationships, and worldly pleasures. Like the prodigal son in the Bible, I've come to the end of myself. None of my seeking or striving has brought me any closer to the desires of my heart. I confess that there have been times I resented the search itself; times I have been angry at my own emptiness and my inability to quench it.*

*I'm ready to stop struggling, God. I'm ready to stop looking around every corner, behind every door, to any habit or human being to satisfy my longings. I believe that everything I want is found in You. I want to know You. In faith, I accept the sacrifice of Your Son Jesus Christ as the payment for my sin. In faith, I ask Him to come and live in me, making me into the whole and healthy person I long to be. I call on His name to save me, and I believe there is no other name that can.*

*I understand that this is just the beginning of my brand new life. I look forward to the process of becoming like You, Jesus—and to the day when I will see You face to face. When I do, I know that it will be worth any pain I might endure here and that every hour of searching will be rewarded a hundredfold when I hear You say, "Well done." From now on, I want to play my life out before an audience of One—and to seek Your approval before anyone else's.*

*"As the deer pants for the water brooks, so my soul pants for Thee, O God. My soul thirsts for God, for the living God; When shall I come and appear before God?" (Ps. 42:1–2, NASB). I am waiting for the day. Amen.*

# Heaven Rules
## The Penny of Humility

*Humility . . . is simply*
*the sense of entire nothingness;*
*which comes when we see how truly God is all,*
*and in which we make way for God to be all.*
—Andrew Murray

When I was saved as a fourteen year old, I was radically saved. My life changed in tangible ways. I quit drinking. I stopped using drugs. I tried to follow Jesus and to tell others about Him so that they could experience the incredible power and forgiveness of God too. I was as sold out to Him as I had been to the world—and I didn't hide it for a minute. All the things "good Christians" do, I began to do with a passion. I prayed. I read the Bible. I led others to the Lord. But now I know that more important than what a believer might do *for* God is the work God does *in* him or her. "We are not meant to be illuminated versions," Oswald Chambers said, "but the common stuff of ordinary life exhibiting the marvel of the grace of God. The great hindrance in spiritual life is that we will look for great things to do. 'Jesus took a towel . . . and began to wash the disciples' feet.'"

Many who follow Christ mistakenly strive after the "high water marks" of the Christian experience—power, boldness, zeal, service, self-sacrifice—and never discover the sweeter graces of meekness, humility, lowliness, and servanthood. These are the graces that brought Him from heaven—and the ones He brought with Him when He came. Such old-fashioned virtues are certainly not encouraged by the world—and sometimes not even by our brothers and sisters in the faith. They're looked upon as oddities at best, and at worst, as weaknesses. Nevertheless, Paul encouraged his new converts at Philippi to model them, saying:

> *Have this attitude in yourselves which was also in Christ Jesus, who, although He existed in the form of God, did not regard equality with God a thing to be grasped, but emptied Himself, taking the form of a bond-servant, and being made in the likeness of men. And being found in appearance as a man, He humbled Himself by becoming obedient to the point of death, even death on a cross (Phil. 2:5-9, NASB).*

There was no pride in the Lord Jesus Christ, but there was plenty in Rick Amato. As a high school student, I excelled in athletics. I worked at it, shaping my body for peak performance. I was known as a long-ball hitter in baseball, and I made a reputation for myself as a fearless football player. Wrestling was another arena where my size and strength paid off, and I took great satisfaction in the honors I won on the mat. I had the attitude of a jock, complete with the chest-out strut; but soon after I was saved, something began to change.

No one had told me that Christians were supposed to be humble. I am Italian—and Italian men are taught to walk with their heads held high. But I knew almost instinctively that a change was required. I began to remind myself to look down—to get my chin out of the air and to eye the ground. In fact, that's how I started finding real pennies, gravity being what it is. I'm sure I passed by plenty of them before, but now I saw them, and they began to remind me of the loving Father who has scattered "spiritual pennies" my way since the day we met.

Some folks confuse humility with self-condemnation, but the two are worlds apart. For the believer, it's not our own sin that ultimately humbles us, it's the overwhelming grace and goodness of Almighty God. His kindness leads us to repentance, and His mercy shatters our pride. He prizes humility in His people. *"For My hand made all these things,"* He said through the prophet Isaiah, *"thus all these things came into being. . . . But to this one I will look, To Him who is humble and contrite of spirit, and who trembles at My word"* (Isa. 66:2, NASB). In our humanistic age, the distinctions between Creator and creature have become tragically blurred, but God has not changed. He is immutable—"the ever-living, ever-present, ever-acting One who upholdeth all things by the word of His power; and in whom all things exist." [1]

So I started walking in a different way. But physical posture was just the beginning of what I needed to learn about the practice of humility. I soon discovered a man's internal stance before God and his fellow men is not so easily trained as his body and that God will use whatever means He chooses to guard one of His own from pride— even pain.

## *Early Blessings*

Like high school seniors everywhere, I was beginning to be concerned about what would follow graduation. I prayed regularly for God's guidance about attending college—asking whether He wanted me to go, and if He did, where did He want me to go? In the course of one evening, I received back-to-back phone calls from two unexpected "recruiters." Tennessee Temple University was looking at my buddy Norman Maurer for their basketball program, and Norm put in a word for me too. One night as I was wrestling over these issues in prayer, my father knocked on the door and said, "Son, you've got a phone call." It was Ron Bishop from Temple saying they'd like to talk to me about attending there. I told him that I was praying hard about what I should do and would certainly consider their program.

Then as soon as I hung up the phone, it rang again. I never even got my hand off the receiver.

"Hello?"

"Is this Rick Amato?" a deep voice asked.

"Speaking," I said.

"Rick, this is Jerry Falwell. You may know me from television . . ."

"Well, no," I responded naively, "I don't watch much TV."

"Well, I've heard about you," he said, "and I believe that if basketball players deserve scholarships, then young preachers do too. If you're interested in attending Liberty University, son, I think we can arrange it even if Norm doesn't come here."

I did attend Liberty University, and to this day believe it was truly God who led me there. School was difficult for me, though, and it took me a long time to get my degree. I married Nancy, my high school sweetheart, and we began our family while I was still struggling to graduate. But in my time at Liberty, God began to work in my life in exciting ways. He put people in my path who needed Christ and let me see their lives changed by Him. He allowed me to preach and proclaim the good news of Jesus Christ during the good times and the bad. I desperately wanted to serve Him, and He provided me with so many opportunities. Whatever else was going on, He was clearly leading me into full-time evangelism and blessing those early evangelistic messages with many converts. I could not have been more overjoyed than I was to follow Him in that direction.

## A Painful Message

It's possible to get so involved in the work of God that you forget God Himself. I know from experience. Between studying, preaching, and being a full-time husband and father, I found myself spread thin—but unwilling to slow down and take time to rekindle my first love. Eventually, I was in full-blown rebellion. It's true that I was involved in things that were benefitting others, but I was compromising my own spiritual and physical health in the process. God had to get my attention, and to do it, he used what C. S. Lewis called "God's megaphone": pain.

One day I noticed that my stomach was hurting. When the pain persisted, I saw a doctor. He ran some tests and said he would call me when the results were available. By the time I got home from his office, he had already phoned, and when I called him back, his words surprised me.

"Rick," he said, "you need to come right back to the hospital."

I laughed. "I don't have time to do that right now," I told him. "I have a lot of important things to take care of."

He wasn't budging. "Nothing you have to do could be more important than what I'm about to tell you. Your white blood cell count is 19,500."

"So? Is that bad?" I questioned.

"21,000 and you might be a corpse," he said.

I went back to the hospital and was promptly admitted. A few days later, Christmas Day, a team of grim-faced doctors stood by my bed.

"We've discovered a very large mass in your abdomen," they told me. "We don't know what it is. We're going to do an exploratory laparotomy and cut it out. But that's not our chief concern."

*Great,* I thought. *I have a mass the size of two and a half grapefruits growing inside me, and that's the good news.*

"What exactly do you mean?" I asked.

"You've developed peritonitis, Rick," one of the doctors said. "It's an infection of the lining of your intestines, and that means you're a very sick man. I don't want to alarm you, but I would frankly suggest that you get your affairs in order, just in case."

I was so stunned by what I was hearing that I didn't really respond. But when the doctors left the room, tears quickly welled up in my eyes. I prayed, "God, You don't understand. I'm Rick Amato. I'm twenty-six years old. I have a wife and five children. I'm going to preach the gospel to the world. Please, God. You don't understand."

Then I heard *His* still, small voice: "No Rick, *you* don't understand. I am a holy and jealous God. And if I can't have you, heart and soul, then no one can."

As I lay there in that room, I thought back on the way I'd once loved Jesus. He had been my consuming passion. *Him*—not work for Him. The only prayer that came to my lips for days was this: "Oh, God, please have mercy."

Three days later I woke up from surgery to find a tube in my throat, two tubes in my arms, two in my side, and a catheter in my groin. There was a large incision in my abdomen where the surgeons had removed ten inches of my colon, then rerouted a portion of it outside my body and connected it to a plastic pouch. I learned that this procedure is called a colostomy. And I learned that a colostomy patient can change that bag up to ten times a day or more.

I was lucky to be alive, and I knew it. But the set of emotional and financial circumstances I hit head-on when I left the hospital was almost as frightening as the prospect of an early death had been. I had no health insurance and no life insurance. The medical bills from my surgery were staggering. In a matter of weeks, my young family was destitute. We ended up living on welfare benefits and were eventually evicted from our home. Our car was repossessed. In my sickness and discouragement, I began to wonder if it wouldn't have been better for me to die.

## Falling in Love Again

One day my father came to see me. Although Dad had struggled with his own mental health for years, he had always tried to teach me to believe in God. He also taught me that strong men are loving men. He was divorced from my mother by this time and living hundreds of miles away. When he showed up at the hospital, I knew I was in trouble. There I lay, sick, broke, frightened, and humiliated. He took my hand and held it like he had when I was a little boy. I loved him so much! When he finally spoke, there were tears in his eyes.

"Son," he said, "Jesus said it would be better to go through life maimed than to miss His plan and have your whole body thrown into hell. To have no hands or eyes or feet would be better than that. You have a physical problem—but I'd rather see you wear that bag for the rest of your life and truly love and serve Him than be perfectly well in your body and sick in your soul. It's better for you to have a colostomy bag and love Jesus than to be physically whole and not really love Him."

His words rang true. My ambitions for God were so big. I wanted to do great things for the kingdom. I wanted to preach the gospel to corners of the world I had never even seen. I was just a street kid from Detroit, but I had big dreams. The trouble was, I had become more in love with them than I was with the One who inspired them. Now I faced a choice. Maybe I couldn't preach. But I could pray. Maybe I would never address another congregation, but I could talk to the man or woman on the corner. I might not ever get my degree, but I could be His student for the rest of my life.

Once my priorities were reordered, a wonderful thing happened. I fell in love with Jesus again. In the days to come I would have brand new opportunities to serve Him.

## A New Beginning

Throughout history, God has been a deliverer. From the earliest days of Israel He has loved, led, and rescued His people. *"They wandered in the wilderness,"* the psalmist wrote, *"in a desert region; They did not find a way to an inhabited city. They were hungry and thirsty; Their soul fainted within them. Then they cried out to the LORD in their trouble; He delivered them out of their distresses"* (Ps. 107:4-6, NASB). God has always been a deliverer and man has always been a wanderer, prone at the first sign of ease to leave the protective arms of God and strike out on his own. *"Because they had rebelled against the words of God, And spurned the counsel of the Most High. Therefore He humbled their heart with labor; They stumbled and there was none to help"* (Ps. 107:11-12, NASB).

When God delivers, we sometimes foolishly begin to trust in our own self-sufficiency and not in His mercy and loving-kindness. Pride—even subtle pride—is the result, and it is incredibly dangerous. Instead, we need to be constantly aware that any ease or good we might experience is simply a result of His grace—not of our ability or skill or striving. "The life of saved ones," wrote Andrew Murray, "must needs bear this stamp of deliverance from sin, and full restoration to their original state; their whole relation to God and man marked by an all-pervading humility. Without this there can be no true abiding in God's presence, or experience of His favor and the power of His spirit; without this no abiding faith or love or strength."[2]

A call from Reverend Lloyd Locklear, pastor of a Free Will Baptist church, came shortly after I decided that if God never wanted me to preach again, I could live with that reality. Lloyd is a full-blooded Lumbee Indian who leads one of the downriver Detroit area's largest churches. He had been the only minister in Detroit who stood by me—at a time when I didn't even know him. He invited me to speak, and quite honestly, I hesitated. Not out of humility—

but because my own views were rather narrow at the time. I felt that my particular denominational convictions were correct, naturally, and I told him so.

"I couldn't possibly preach in a Free Will Baptist Church," I finally admitted.

"Why not," he asked? "We love Jesus, too."

"Besides," I continued, "my ministry is over."

With a knowing smile, Lloyd said, "That's right. But God's is just beginning."

I thought about that a moment and then reconsidered. "Why not?" I agreed.

I will never forget that particular preaching "assignment." I may not have been one hundred percent sure I was right in accepting it, but God confirmed His presence in a mighty way. The Holy Spirit was there in that church in power, and the next thing I knew, I was getting calls from other churches, inviting me to preach. People were coming to the Lord, I was making enough money to begin to dig out of debt, and slowly I started coming out of the depression of the past months. I teamed up with some godly laymen to form RAM—Rick Amato Ministries—during this time, with the goal of preaching the gospel to the world.

## Seeing the "Specialist"

The one thing that had not changed since my illness was the fact that I still had to deal with the effects of my colostomy. I was still wearing the bag and had never quite adjusted to the reality of it. I went back to the doctor and tried to convince him to remove it, but after consulting with other specialists and ordering more tests, he refused.

"You're going to have to wear a colostomy bag for the rest of your life, Rick," he said. "You'd better get used to it."

"Why can't you just put me back together?" I asked.

"I can't do that. You have Crohn's disease. It's an incurable, degenerative disease of the bowels. Our biopsies have confirmed it. I'm sorry. The bag is a must. Permanently."

I was not satisfied. I wanted to be well—and I did not want to live with a debilitating disease. I needed time to think, to process all that had happened to me, so I took a few days off and headed for Bailey Island, Maine. Bailey Island is one of my favorite places on earth. My uncle, George Johnson, is a lobsterman there, and it was the perfect place for me to retreat and be alone with God. There, with the North Atlantic thundering beside me, I walked and thought and prayed.

"Lord," I prayed, "You've taught me so much. I will love You and fear You for the rest of my life, no matter what. But God, I've been preaching 'by His stripes we are healed,' and I need that healing. You've touched my soul—now God, please, touch my body." In the moments that followed, with only the cry of gulls and the sound of the sea in my ears, I clearly heard the voice of God. It wasn't an audible voice, but a sure, gentle whisper in my heart: "Don't worry about what the specialists have said. I am the specialist." I went inside and told my beautiful and loving Aunt Norma Jean what God had said, and I was surprised at her faith. She believed me.

Then I called Nancy in Detroit; I could hardly wait to tell her what I'd heard. When she answered the phone, she said, "What's that screeching noise in the background?"

"Sea gulls," I said. "Nancy, I think I've been healed."

"You've been healed?" she asked.

"That's right, I've been healed," I said with more certainty. "Look, here's what I want you to do. I want you to call the University of Michigan and set up an appointment for me with Dr. Keith Henley there. He's an expert in gastroenterology. Can you do that?"

"Oh, Rick," Nancy said, "please don't do this to yourself. You're in for a big letdown. You're going from doctor to doctor, and you're spending all this money. Don't do it, Rick. You're getting your hopes up for no reason. God will give you the grace to wear the bag. Can't you accept it as His will for your life?"

No one desired my healing more than my wife. She saw every day the frustration I experienced dealing with the colostomy. But she knew that if God chose it, He would give me the grace to live with it. I believed that then. I believe it now. But I also knew what I had heard, and so I pressed her. "Nancy, please. Just call him. I'm telling you—I've really been healed."

She did as I asked. I left Bailey Island, and she was waiting at the airport for me when I arrived in Detroit. We went directly to the University Hospital, where Dr. Henley examined me. He ran more tests. He did biopsies. Finally, he had all the information he needed, and he called me into his office.

"Sit down, Mr. Amato," he said.

I couldn't. I was too anxious to hear what the tests had shown. "I don't need to sit down," I told him.

"Sit down, Mr. Amato," he repeated.

I sat down. "Who told you that you have Crohn's disease?" he asked.

I told him the names of the specialists I had seen at William Beaumont and Oakwood hospitals in Detroit.

"Did they do biopsies?" he asked.

"Yes."

"First, let me say that the physicians you mentioned are fine doctors. I have the utmost respect for them. But nothing that I've seen confirms their diagnosis. You don't have Crohn's disease. In fact, you don't have any disease at all," he said.

Although I believed in my heart that I was healed, I still questioned him further. "Maybe it's in remission," I suggested. "Crohn's disease can go into remission, can't it?"

"It can," he said, "but if the disease was in remission, you would have scar tissue, and there is none. Your bowels look just like a baby's bowels."

I sat there for a moment taking in what he was saying. No disease. No evidence of it ever having been present. Needless to say, the colostomy bag was soon removed. I praise God that, to this day, no problems have recurred with my colon. He did, in fact, heal my body from a condition that was daily made obvious to me and others by the bag. It had been under my clothing, sure, but it was there. I knew it, and others who knew about my diagnosis knew it. He "detached" me from it by eliminating the need for it. It is a powerful miracle—and it illustrates an even more powerful lesson that I will never forget.

We have a disease, you and I. It's called pride. We're born with it. And just like the colostomy, the effects of it are with us every day. We know it. Others know it. We can cover it up, disguise it, or pretend it isn't there—but that won't make it go away. The only thing that can deliver us from our sin disease is a touch from the One who "specializes" in removing it: His name is Jesus. He is the healer. I could not reverse the effects of my colostomy or heal my Crohn's disease anymore than I can change my sin nature or give myself a new heart. Only Jesus can do that.

Once He does deliver us from our sin, the biggest mistake you or I can make is to think we no longer need Him. The truth is, our dependence on God has only just begun. He does not save us so that we will become independent, autonomous, on-top-of-it-all Christians. His goal for us is that we be conformed to the image of Jesus Christ, and Jesus was a humble, gentle Savior.

But humility isn't popular today. Today, you and I live in a culture that celebrates bigness. Everyone who's anyone is famous. Anything worth having is fabulous. Bigger is better. Less is not more, it's less. Only more is more, and everyone wants more. We live in the age of hype, and it's not easy to determine who and what is for real. Sometimes well-meaning people introduce me with flowery words and laudatory phrases, and I just want to say, "Won't somebody say that I love Jesus? Isn't it enough that my soul is afire for God?"

God did not call you and me to become famous, fabulous, or fantastic. He just called us to be faithful. Nowhere in God's Word does it say that at the end of life's race He will greet us with the words "Well done, thou good and famous servant." No promise of "Well done, thou good and fabulous servant," or even, "Well done, thou good and fantastic servant." No. The words we press on to hear are these: "Well done, thou good and faithful servant." God will not search our "stuff" to see if we deserve His fellowship for eternity—He will search our hearts. Our stuff may impress the world, but it is our humility before Him—and our total reliance on Jesus Christ and Him crucified—that pleases God most.

The apostle Paul understood this when he wrote to the Philippians:

> We are the true circumcision, who worship in the Spirit of God and glory in Christ Jesus and put no confidence in the flesh, although I myself might have confidence even in the flesh. If anyone else has a mind to put confidence in the flesh, I far more: circumcised the eighth day, of the nation of Israel, of the tribe of Benjamin, a Hebrew of Hebrews; as to the Law, a Pharisee; as to zeal, a persecutor of the church; as to the righteousness which is in the Law, found blameless. But whatever things were gain to me, those things I have counted as loss for the sake of Christ. More than that, I count all things to be loss in view of the surpassing value of knowing Christ Jesus my Lord, for whom I have suffered the loss of all things, and count them but rubbish in order that I may gain Christ (Phil. 3:3-8, NASB).

God blessed me at a young age with so much. He called and equipped me to preach the cross of Jesus Christ. He gave me a beautiful wife and five wonderful children. He used me to bring others to a saving knowledge of Christ. He answered my prayers and made dreams come true in ways that were truly supernatural. And then with His "megaphone" of pain He gave the penny of humility—and like Paul, I have come to count everything but what Jesus did for me as loss. It is less than nothing; but with Christ Jesus, nothing is everything.

"Let us," wrote Andrew Murray, "at the very commencement of our meditations, admit that there is nothing so natural to man, nothing so insidious and hidden from our sight, nothing so difficult and dangerous as pride. Let us feel that nothing but a very determined and persevering waiting on God and Christ will discover how lacking we are in the grace of humility, and how impotent to obtain what we seek. Let us study the character of Christ until our souls are filled with the love and admiration of His lowliness. And let us believe that, when we are broken down under a sense of our pride, and our impotence to cast it out, Jesus Christ Himself will come to impart this grace, too, as part of His wondrous life within us."

Humility is a penny I first discovered through pain, but it is a grace I continue to seek to receive as I walk—not like a cocky high school jock or a hard-driving preacher of the cross but as a broken man who owes everything he has and is to the Lord Jesus Christ. "Jesus paid it all, all to Him I owe." Heaven rules.

# A Prayer for Humility

*Heavenly Father, I praise You and lift up Your name. You revealed Yourself to Abraham as El Shaddai, the Almighty One.*

*Almighty God, I need the miracle of humility in my life. Even as I ask for this grace, I realize how foreign it is to my spirit. Pride, not humility, is at the very heart of me. Out of Your great goodness, please make known to me and take from my heart every kind and form and degree of pride—whether from evil spirits or my own corrupt nature. Please awaken in me the deepest depth of the humility that makes me a vessel of Your light and Your truth. In my surest moments, God, I know that You are all that's good in me—and that anything I might hold up to the world as gain is really only loss.*

*I confess that I have tried in my own strength to be humble and am ashamed to find that even this becomes a source of pride in me! I yield all that I am and ever hope to be to You right now. Here's my heart, Lord— every secret part. Take it and make it like the heart of the meek and lowly Lamb of God, in whose name and gentle spirit I come. Amen.*

# Prayer *Is* Power

## The Penny of Prevailing Prayer

> *Remember the longer the blessing is coming,*
> *the richer it will be when it arrives.*
> *The blessing which costs us the most prayer*
> *will be worth the most.*
> —Charles Spurgeon

It never occurred to me not to pray. When I became a Christian as a teenager, I became a praying Christian, and God showed me almost immediately that there is great power in prayer. As a consequence, I believe strongly in going to God with everything—large or small. If we consulted God about the kind of clothes that we wear, I believe we might all dress more modestly. If we consulted Him about the money we spend, I believe we might spend it more wisely. God is vitally interested in all that concerns us.

## Power to Meet Needs

God teaches us about the power of prayer right where we are. When I look back on some of my early prayers, I am humbled by their simplicity and decidedly "unchurchy" content. But God honored many of them as this chapter will show. I remember a fishing expedition with my high school buddy Norman, when, for some reason, we decided to take no food along. Like real outdoorsmen, we were planning to cook and eat only what we caught, and by the end of the day, we were starving! From 6:00 in the morning to 6:00 at night, neither of us had had so much as a nibble on our lines.

As we were rowing back into shore we prayed. "Lord," we said, "we're hungry. We don't want a whole lot of fish, just enough to feed us for tonight. Please, Lord, give us some fish." The sun was beginning to set, and the bugs were coming out. But we had prayed, so we decided to give it one more try. We turned the boat around, and about twenty strokes out, I saw something flopping around on top of the water. We rowed a little closer and saw a twelve-inch pike struggling there—with a bass almost as big caught in its mouth. The pike was clamped down, and the bass was struggling to get away—but to us, they were dinner!

We easily netted them, took them ashore, filleted them and ate them—our first and only meal of the day. You might think that's one whale of a "fish story," but it's not. It's a prayer story—and it's true. God met our need that day, and in doing so, He taught me a powerful lesson. There is no need that you and I have, no matter how small or seemingly insignificant, that He is not concerned with and able to meet. God has reminded me of that fact more than once.

After our family had weathered a very difficult financial season, we became concerned about our old car, which didn't run well and could barely hold our family of seven. Every time we were out driving, I'd tell my family, "Pray for a station wagon. Pray for a station wagon. Oh, God, give us a station wagon!" On winter mornings when the temperature was twenty below and I was trying to get the car to start, I'd call to the kids, "Hey, you! Are you praying for a station wagon? Pray for a station wagon!" They'd say, "Yeah, Daddy. We did. We did, Daddy."

One night I was preaching in a little church in North Carolina, and, to my amazement, a preacher got right with God. When he did, he also made things right with his brother. A day or two later, he called me and asked me to go with him to see his brother. "Sure," I said, "I'll go with you." So he picked me up and together we drove to what had to be the biggest car lot in North Carolina.

"Your brother works here?" I said, making conversation.

He nodded. "My brother owns here."

We went inside, and the preacher introduced me to his brother, Phil Gandy, explaining that I had been the person who led him back to the Lord.

The brother smiled broadly. "You know," he said, "you've done a lot for this family. What kind of car do you drive?"

"It's a '79 Granada with terminal cancer," I said.

He said, "Why don't you go out to the lot and pick out a nice van for your family. I'd be happy to work out a good price."

"I don't need a van," I said, "but you've got a 1984 Chevy station wagon out there. I'd like that if you can work a good deal on it."

He seemed shocked. "You'd really rather have a used wagon than a new van?"

"Yes, sir," I said, "I would."

He looked at me curiously, then instructed a nearby employee: "Get the title and the keys to the Caprice and *give* it to this guy."

The Amato kids' prayers had scored big time. This station wagon was not new, but it had electric seats, electric windows, tilt steering wheel, cruise control, AM/FM stereo *and* air conditioning. More than all that, it was a direct provision for my family's need from the hand of Almighty God.

Jesus taught His disciples to pray for daily needs by asking for a day's supply of bread. You or I can simply drive to the supermarket and purchase a loaf—and usu-

ally some bologna or peanut butter to put between it—
but for the man or woman in Jesus' day, bread actually
meant survival. It was a necessity, not a menu option.
What He did not encourage them to pray for was tomorrow's bread. Instead, He said, *"Therefore do not be anxious
for tomorrow; for tomorrow will care for itself. Each day has
enough trouble of its own"* (Matt. 6:34, NASB).

While God is deeply concerned about our needs,
tomorrow's bread is not a need . . . until tomorrow. And
twenty-four hours can change everything. Why don't we
need tomorrow's bread? Because we may not be here
tomorrow. Because Jesus may return today. Because, like
the children of Israel, we must come to see God and God
alone as the supplier of our every need. When Israel was
in the wilderness of Sinai on the way to the promised
land, God fed the people daily with manna. And manna
was a perishable food staple. It was only good for a day.
In fact, God instructed the Israelites not to store it because
it would go bad. (They tried. It did.) They could not
collect a week's supply and congratulate themselves on
their thriftiness because more than they needed bread,
they needed to know that their provider was Yahweh
God.

Prayer is part of God's plan in providing for our
needs. But you and I need to ask for the mind of Christ in
determining what our needs truly are. God is, and always
has been, more concerned with our spiritual health than
He is with our material wealth. Still, He stands ready to
meet our real needs in loving response to our prayers.

## *Power to Effect Change*

Years before the collapse of the former Soviet Union,
I stood in front of a world map and prayed with great
passion for the people of Russia. I had a list of names—
hundreds of names I could hardly pronounce—provided
by Transworld Radio, of men and women imprisoned for
their beliefs in that Communist country. I thought about

the atheism that had paralyzed the Russian people for more than seventy years, and my heart broke. There were many times that I wept as I stood before the map and spoke their names. I was not a well-known evangelist at the time. I was a young preacher from Detroit, Michigan, with a burden on my heart from God. So I prayed. "Lord, set these men and women free. God, honor their loyalty to You. Send the Word of God to them. Break down the regime that holds many of them fast in atheism."

I was so committed to prayer for this part of the world that I checked books out of the library on Russia, which puzzled the librarian who knew that I was Italian. I'd say, "Yes, I know, but someday I'm going to Russia to preach the gospel." I meant it.

It seems strange today to tell you that. But it is true. And in my prayers for change, I learned that God is the God of history, and that He and He alone has the power to change it. The entire world watched as the Berlin Wall fell, the Soviet Union collapsed, and the nations of Eastern Europe emerged from behind the Iron Curtain. Not knowing the real truth, newscasters, reporters, politicians, and heads of state have given their opinions about what caused these dramatic world events. But the real story is the "greatest story never told," and it will only be completely understood from eternity's perspective. I believe in my heart that God, in response to the prayers of His people, set these nations free. Nothing that is written in the media or the history books will ever convince me otherwise.

When I went to the Soviet Union for the first time in 1990, I traveled with a man named Vernon Brewer, who had been smuggling Bibles into Russia for years. We took 10,000 copies of the Scriptures with us on that trip and distributed every one of them, which was a miracle. But as far as I'm concerned the real miracle of the trip came in an ill-smelling Communist high-rise at nearly midnight, when I went to an "unsanctioned" Soviet church. As my eyes adjusted to the dim light, I saw men crowded shoulder-to-shoulder on makeshift pews (two-by-fours stretched between chairs), emaciated and sallow-skinned from the radioactive water and molded bread they had eaten for years in Siberian camps. And then I heard their names—names that had been on my lips hundreds of times, year after year, from thousands of miles away—and I knew that prayer is power.

These men, whose crimes—printing New Testaments and owning Bibles—had imprisoned them, had been set free by the prayers of the saints and the power of God! Even today, when you stand in Red Square in the heart of Moscow, you will see on your left the tower of the Kremlin and the red star of Communism, and on the right (reaching even higher) the spire of Saint Basil's cathedral—and on top of it, a shimmering cross. Prayer is power—and it changes things!

## Power to Grow

I'm convinced that prayer is the only way to grow as a Christian. God says His plan for you and me is that we become like His Son, Jesus Christ. But that can be a slow process for many of us. Whether we struggle with unmet needs, inadequate finances, a dark past, or an uncertain future—the answer is in prayer. And when we neglect prayer, we stop growing.

When I was a new Christian, I read the Bible like a starving man devours food. One day, I came upon this familiar passage:

> ". . . Our Father, who art in heaven, Hallowed be Thy Name. Thy kingdom come, Thy will be done, On earth as it is in heaven. Give us this day our daily bread. And forgive us our debts, as we also have forgiven our debtors. And do not lead us into temptation, but deliver us from evil. For Thine is the kingdom, and the power, and the glory, forever. . ." (Matt. 6:9-13, NASB).

As I read I felt as if God were right there with me. That I could ask anything in the world and receive it. Strangely enough, the first thing that came to mind to ask for was a wallet. Why? I didn't have one. It was that simple. So I said, "Lord, please give me a wallet. Amen."

A short time later I was hitchhiking and a fellow stopped to give me a ride. After we'd driven a few blocks, he said, "Open the box on the seat there, next to you." I don't know if you've ever been to Detroit, but I was reaching for the door handle, not the box! I thought, *Oh, no! A nut case has picked me up.*

"Go on, kid," he said, "open it."

I said, "No, that's okay. Thanks anyway."

Frustrated by this time, he ripped the cover off the box, and inside were literally dozens of—you guessed it—wallets.

"Where did you get these?" I said. I was pretty sure he wasn't a serial killer, but I wasn't sure just what else he might be. "Are you an angel?" I asked.

Now it was his turn to think I was crazy.

"No," he said, "I'm an insurance salesman, and they're free samples. Take as many as you want."

I took two and promptly lost them both. But the next time I went to church, Bill Hall, my friend Marty's father, called me aside. He was a man who had seen potential in me and had been involved in my conversion. He said, "Son, a few days ago, the Holy Spirit told me to buy this. I didn't know who it was for. But when I saw you today, I knew it was for you." Then he handed me a beautiful leather wallet. Engraved on it were the words of the Lord's Prayer, the same words God had used to inspire me to ask Him for something only days before. My eyes misted over as I read them: *"Our Father, Who art in heaven . . ."*

Prayer and God's answers to it grow us up in our faith in a way that little else can. That was one of my first experiences with answered prayer, but it hasn't been the last by a long shot. No matter what kind of trouble I've passed through since then, one thing is sure: prayer has been the channel of God's blessings and the source of all power in my life. I've seen its results time and again, and every time, my faith has grown.

## Power to Persevere

Prayer not only meets needs, changes circumstances, and fosters our growth—prayer has the power to help us persevere when life is tough. Consider Sid Bream's story. Sid Bream was a first baseman for the Pittsburgh Pirates and is now playing for the Houston Astros. In between, he put in three great seasons with the Atlanta Braves, leading them on and off the field to three league championships and two World Series appearances. Sid is a fine Christian man, and in his five seasons with the Pirates he became very popular with the Pittsburgh fans. He is also a good friend.

One day while he was still with the Pirates, Sid spoke at a meeting with me. When the meeting was over, he gave me his honorarium. "Sid," I said, "this is so generous. Man, what can I do for you?"

"Pray for me," he said.

I did. Every day I prayed for Sid Bream. I prayed that Sid would always put God first in his life and that he would get to play in a World Series before the end of his career. A month or so later, I received a call from Sid, and he sounded very agitated. "Man," he said, "have you been praying for me? I asked you to pray for me."

"I have been," I said. "Why?"

"I just injured my knee, and it's bad," he said. With that, Sid's wife, Michelle, came on the line.

"Rick," Michelle said, "Sid's really upset. I'm sorry. I'd better go. I'll talk to you later, okay?" She hung up the phone.

I continued praying every day for Sid. I prayed that he would continue to keep seeking God and that he would reach the World Series. Two months went by before I received another call from Michelle. "Rick," she said, "Sid's doing great. We've had a spiritual revival in our home. He realizes that baseball isn't everything—and we're really seeking the Lord." Sid was right, of course. Long after baseball careers and the money they produce are gone, our relationship with God will continue. But that wasn't the end of the story.

Sid became a free agent later that year, and the Pirates did not pick up his contract—a move that was very unpopular with Pittsburgh fans. He went to the Atlanta Braves, instead. (On his first at-bat as a Brave at Pittsburgh's Three Rivers Stadium, the fans there gave him a five-minute standing ovation—then rose to their feet again when he tipped his hat, stepped into the box, and popped a home run over the center field wall!) Sid Bream went to the World Series that year as an Atlanta Brave. And he went again the next year.

Sid has had the same knee operated on five times in the course of his career, but that didn't stop the Houston Astros from trading for him when his contract with Atlanta expired. Whatever you are struggling with today, don't be too quick to conclude that it is bad. Sid Bream has a bad knee, and it's taken him to the World Series—twice. Sometimes the worst things that happen to us turn out to be blessings in disguise if we'll just pray for the strength to persevere.

Our High Priest—the One who goes before God on our behalf—faced the darkest night of His earthly life alone, as He prayed *"not My will, but Thine be done" (Luke 22:42, NASB)*. In the garden of Gethsemane, He asked for the strength to finish what He knew lay just ahead—and God provided it. His life seemed to end in tragedy on a Judean hillside, but the darkest day in history was simply a door to the glory of His resurrection. Prayer has in it the very power to persevere.

## Powerful Lessons in Prayer

My son Joseph has a baseball card I know he'll never trade. It's a 1993 card that features a picture of Lee Guetterman, pitcher for the New York Mets. You might think it's not too valuable, but you'd be wrong.

In March of 1993, Lee called me to tell me that he'd been sent from the New York Mets down to a minor league team in Kentucky. His wife Drew and I claimed the promise of Matthew 18:19, *"If two of you agree on earth about anything that they may ask, it shall be done for them by My Father who is in heaven" (NASB)*, agreeing that Lee would be back in the majors by June 30 of that same year. Lee called again in mid-June to tell me that he'd been released by the minor league team, and could stay or go home. He said he decided to stay, adding, "If I leave baseball, it will be because God sent me out." I remember wishing I had his faith.

On Tuesday evening, the twenty-ninth of June, I went to bed full of doubts. "Tomorrow's the thirtieth," I thought, "and Guetterman's finished." Oh, ye of little faith! The next morning dawned with a phone call from Drew. "Rick," she said, "Lee got a call from the St. Louis Cardinals at 1:00 this morning. He's on a plane to St. Louis, and he's pitching tonight!" All on June 30th.

Later that day, my son Joseph and I went down to the gas station to get a soda. (Sometimes we guys just have to get away, you know?) I told Joe to get a soda, nothing else, but he came back out breathless—with a soda and a package of baseball cards. I was just about to launch into a speech about doing what you're told until I saw the top card on the pack he was holding out to me: it was Lee Guetterman. Now what do you think the odds of him getting that card, on that day, at that place, were, with all the millions of baseball cards there must be floating around?

Well, actually, I'd say pretty good. You see, you and I have a God who knows when sparrows fall and the number of hairs on our heads— and when your son will be the next person to pick up a pack of baseball cards. Nothing misses His notice. Nothing. It's not just any baseball card, you see. It's confirmation that we have a God who answers prayer!

Some answers to prayer seem to be almost immediate, and at other times, days, weeks, months, years go by with no word from God. But, as Charles Spurgeon said, "That which is gained speedily by a single prayer is sometimes only a second-rate blessing; but that which is gained after many a desperate tug and many an awful struggle, is a full weighted and precious blessing." Nancy and I received just such a blessing not long ago.

When I was at Liberty University trying to complete my education, we met a young lady who had once starred on the soap opera "Days of Our Lives." She asked us to pray for her boyfriend in Beverly Hills, saying, "I've been born again, and he thinks I've joined a cult. He needs Jesus. His name is Mark Hudson."

Every time we prayed with her, she'd remind Nancy and me to pray for Mark Hudson. "Please don't forget to pray for Mark Hudson," she said over and over again. For several years we prayed. Then we returned to Detroit, lost contact with her, and quite honestly, forgot about Mark, too. A few years went by, and Nancy and I happened to be in Los Angeles, holding a revival service. We had two hours to kill the day we were to leave, and Nancy said, "Hey, Rick! Let's go to Beverly Hills and see how the rich and famous live!"

We did. We drove up and down some fabulous-looking streets but never saw anyone famous. As we were scouting another neighborhood, Nancy pointed to a guy outside his house watering his roses, and said "Why don't you pull over and ask him?"

"I'm not asking him anything," I said.

"Come on Rick, ask him," she said. Nancy has a special way of reasoning with me. I pulled the car over, rolled down the window, and rather embarrassed, said "Excuse me. Excuse me. Sir?"

The guy looked a little puzzled. "Yes?"

Then I asked, as only a tourist from Detroit could, "Hey, I was wondering, could you tell me where some rich and famous people live?"

He laughed immediately. "Well," he said, "depends on what you mean by rich and famous." We struck up a conversation, and I shared some gospel literature with him and explained I was an evangelist in town to preach a church service. "My name's Rick Amato," I finally said.

"Well, Rick," he said, "it's nice to meet you. I'm a band director for Joan Rivers' late-night talk show, and my name's *Mark Hudson*." I promise you, that's exactly what the man said. "My name's Mark Hudson." There are about thirteen million people in the city of Los Angeles, but there was only one that we had prayed for several years: Mark Hudson. We were three thousand miles from home, killing time before a return flight. We had no idea what street we were on, or even that Mark Hudson still lived in L.A. We had all but forgotten about our prayers for Mark, but God hadn't. He remembered. So years later, Nancy and I were allowed to present the gospel to Mark Hudson—at odds of at least thirteen million to one. Prayer is power. It's that simple.

## *You Try It Too!*

There is nothing special about the prayers of Rick Amato. God has demonstrated his power through answered prayer in my life—but I'm just an ordinary person like you. There are no "key phrases" or "magic words" necessary in prayer. We're a lot like that ragtag band of men who followed Jesus and witnessed His incomparable power two thousand years ago. Ordinary folks. Tax accountants. Fishermen. Friends. They watched Him closely—and they saw Him do what no one ever had done before.

They saw Him calm the sea, and said, "What kind of man is this, that even the winds and the sea obey His voice?"

They watched in sheer amazement as He took a little boy's lunch and fed five thousand people, then instructed them to gather the leftovers!

They stood at Lazarus' tomb when He cried, "Come out!" and they saw a dead man walk. Unlimited power streamed from Him, and they knew it. You and I know it too, don't we? Yet, when they asked Him to teach them something, it was not how to calm storms or multiply bread or raise the dead. "Teach us to pray," they said. "Teach us to pray."

I believe they asked Him that because they saw a direct parallel between His public miracles and His private life of prayer. They saw that His one holy obsession was to know God. They observed that He rose up early each morning and began His day by calling on God. That He retreated to be alone with the Father at the end of a grueling day. They saw that the secret to His life was the power of prayer.

When you and I go wrong in prayer, it's not that we pray *incorrectly*. It's that we don't pray at all. Instead, we depend on human scheming and human effort and human aggressiveness and cleverness—and not on the power of God. In a world that champions "personal empowerment," there is not much room left for a power greater than ourselves. We wonder why we are not growing into the image of Christ, why more men and women are not coming to know Jesus Christ, why churches are not full to overflowing. The answer is clear: we're not praying. God says, "They have not because they ask not."

Are you asking? Are you "spending" the penny of prayer each and every day, about matters large and small? Are we listening in silence for His voice? Praising Him for His greatness? Wanting to know more of His ways? C. S. Lewis said prayer did not change God, it changed him. God wants you to know Him, and He wants that knowledge to change you.

He wants you to know the fullness of His power.

He wants you to know the glory of His grace.

He wants you to offer a sacrifice of praise for all that He is and all that He does.

Do you want to be blessed? Don't try to include God in what you're doing—find out what He's doing and do it with Him! Do you want to go someplace? Find out where God's going, and go along! Do you want answered prayer? You can be certain that it's yours when you ask His kingdom to come and His will to be done in your life today. Lord, teach us to pray!

## A Prayer for a Pray-er

*Lord God, You revealed Yourself to Jeremiah as Yahweh Tsidkenu, or "The LORD our righteousness." I exalt that holy name.*

*Many times I don't feel worthy to even talk to You, Father, so I come before You now not in my righteouness but trusting that You, Yahweh Tsidkenu, are my righteousness.*

*God, if I am known as nothing else, let me be known as a person of prayer. Let my communication with You be unhindered by unconfessed sin or wrong attitudes toward my brother. I want to keep a clean slate with You, my heavenly Father, whose approval I long for before anything else. Help me not only to seek Your mind and heart in prayer but to listen to Your voice. Your Son said that His sheep know their Master's voice; give me a hunger to hear the voice I know and then to obey it, regardless of the cost.*

*God, I thank You that You invite our prayers. That You want to talk with us more than we want to talk to You. That You desire a living, daily relationship with those who are Your sons and daughters. Help me to remember that there are many things that are important, but nothing is more important than the time I spend with You at the throne of grace, robed in the righteousness of Your Son, Jesus Christ, in whose name I am privileged to pray. Amen.*

# Walking the
# Narrow Road

## The Penny of Integrity

*In Greece, every stoic was a stoic,*
*but in Christendom, where are the Christians?*
—Friedrich Nietzsche

Last summer my daughters Nancy Jean, Beth Ann and I flew to Moscow. On the first leg of our flight, I was seated next to a man I've admired for a long time. His name is George Anderson, but he's known to baseball fans everywhere as "Sparky." Sparky Anderson is the manager of the Detroit Tigers, and he managed the Cincinnati Reds during their heyday. He's perceived as tough and smart and hardworking—and he certainly is. Sparky was flying to Baltimore, Maryland, for the All-Star game, and our hop from Detroit to Baltimore gave me plenty of time to hear the "gospel according to Sparky."

Many people don't know it, but Sparky Anderson's formal education is quite limited. Still, experience has made him a full-time student of life and of human nature, and he has learned well. Sparky talked to me that day about integrity, and he described two "players" in the game of life that he's observed over and over again. First, he described the "look-in guy." The look-in guy is on the outside of the clubhouse window, looking in. Once he was a winner, in the thick of the action, but then he was sidelined by an injury and doesn't seem to be needed anymore. The look-in guy will get better, and get back in the game. He's not in trouble. The guy in trouble is the one who thinks he doesn't need anyone.

Then Sparky told me about another player he called the "quick-buck guy." The quick-buck guy is the guy who trades what he can't lose for what he can't keep. He's in the game for the now and doesn't think about the future. The quick-buck guy will sell his soul for a few dollars—as long as he can have them *now*.

I was curious as to how this man had built such a reputation among players, owners and fans through the years—so I asked him. "That's easy," he said. "Sparky Anderson doesn't lie." Then he asked me what business I was in, and I told him I was a preacher. Naturally, the conversation turned to integrity in the ministry, and we talked about the fact that many men who have been in places of honor in the ministry have fallen due to character issues. Then Sparky looked at me and said, "Rick, I'm going to give you some advice you can hold onto for the rest of your life: don't sell your soul." Sparky knew, and communicated to me in the short time we were together, that what mattered was to be a man of integrity. That what you are is more important by far than what you may happen to do. That the choices you make matter.

We live in a day when the word of choice is choice. Our culture champions choice. Just a generation or so ago, two people who were sexually intimate were generally married—to each other. Couples who had children were too. People who were sick went to doctors for healing, not help in ending their own lives. Unmarried young women who became pregnant had their children and raised them with help from family and friends or gave them up for adoption to couples who would gladly do so.

But that was a generation ago, and many would say those days were much too confining. We no longer believe in absolutes—we believe in choices. Abortion is not murder, it's a woman's *choice*. Homosexuality is not a sin against the body, it's a life-style *choice*. Sex outside of marriage is certainly not wrong—it's simply a *choice* for two people who may (or may not) be in love. We have freedom that our parents and grandparents never knew— or do we?

Those of you who read this who are Christians will surely say that I've described the world, not the church. But can we tell the difference anymore? Or have those of us who name the name of Jesus become almost indistinguishable from our unbelieving friends, neighbors and coworkers? Researcher George Barna reports that "most Americans possess perspectives on life and spirituality that conform to an orthodox Christian view of the world. Most Americans claim that the Bible is God's Word and is totally accurate in what it teaches. Most believe that sin is still a relevant concept for today's world. The majority indicate that the ten commandments are practical for modern lifestyles. The typical adult concurs that Christianity can supply the answers to today's pressing problems. And most adults believe that prayer has the power to change a person's life."

But while 65 percent of Americans claim to have made a personal commitment to Jesus Christ that is still important to them today, one-third of those who call themselves "born again" believe that all "good" people go to heaven, whether they have embraced Christ or not! And although 56 percent of Americans believe the Bible is the written word of God, only a fraction of them bother to read it.

Do these statistics surprise you? Do they disturb you? They disturb me. I believe we are facing a crisis in the church today that is unprecedented—and it is a crisis of integrity. The gospel of choice may be more popular than ever before in our history, but man has faced choices since Eden. The difference is that today the right to choose is seen as equally important or more important than the choice that is actually made. But Jesus never said, "Follow your heart" or "Follow the crowd" to any of His disciples—He said, "Follow Me." He never said, "Believe what you like"—He said, "Believe in God, believe also in Me." There have always been two "systems" vying for our loyalty: the world's system and God's system. They are not, and have never been, the same. To choose the world is to deny Jesus Christ, and to choose Jesus is to say no to the world.

Instead of implying that they were similar, Jesus contrasted these alternatives clearly: *"Enter by the narrow gate; for the gate is wide, and the way is broad that leads to destruction, and many are those who enter by it. For the gate is small, and the way is narrow that leads to life, and few are those who find it"* (Matt. 7:13-14, NASB). What we desperately need today are men and women of God who will walk the narrow way, men and women of integrity.

## No God on the Broad Road

The best reason I know to walk the narrow road is that Jesus commanded it, and He did so because the broad road is deadly—it leads to destruction. A man cannot be two places at once; if he walks the narrow road, then he will avoid the dangers of the broad road. But the narrow road is not the easy one to travel. On the broad road, a man can do anything he wants to do, have anything he wants to have, feel anything he wants to feel, and act any way he wants to act. Everything in this world waits to accommodate his choices on the broad road. No one says no. The broad road is convenient, comfortable, and crowded. The road signs on it say, "Live Friendly" and "No Danger Ahead." But they lie.

People on the broad road are self-actualized, self-realized, self-satisfied, self-made and self-ish. They go their own way and do their own thing. Their independence is considered by the world to be an asset. They can do whatever they choose, but they cannot do it with God because He is not there. There is no God on the broad road.

And there's something else you need to know about the broad road. You will break down on it. No matter who you are, how rich you become, or how much power you hold over others, you will break down. You might delay or deaden the pain you will encounter with drugs, alcohol, work, or sex, but eventually you will arrive at destruction. On the broad road, no one picks you up when you fall. They can't—because they're running headlong to their own destruction, with their fingers in their ears and their eyes closed.

The Bible tells us a little about the ultimate destination of the travelers on the broad road. They are going to a very real place where God will have the last word. It's a place called hell. Hell is beyond any horror we could imagine. Auschwitz was only a glimpse of it. The catacombs of Rome and the bombed-out streets of Beirut don't hold a candle to its despair. There are those who rationalize that hell is here on earth, or that war is hell, or that poverty is hell. They are wrong. Jesus did not say much about this place, but what He did say is worth considering. He said that hell is so terrible that it would be better to go through life maimed than to end up there. That means it would be better to go through life pushed in a wheelchair, led by a Seeing Eye dog, or fed through a tube than to have your body thrown into hell. You may not believe it, because a lot of people don't, but travelers on the broad road are racing one another to hell.

## The Narrow Road

There is another road for those who choose it. It is extremely narrow by design. Those who travel it must by necessity travel light. There is no room for hatred, malice, pride, greed, prejudice, injustice, or selfishness on the narrow road. It leads to the throne of Almighty God Himself, and He is only interested in the travelers, not their baggage. Life along the narrow road is not perfect, because perfect people don't travel there. It is possible to break down on the narrow road too, to be hurt or to be abused. Sickness and pain are not uncommon—and neither is sin. But the difference in the two roads is this: You are never alone on the narrow road. Never. God is not on the broad road, but He is your constant companion, through His Holy Spirit, on the narrow road.

One day my family and I were riding down the road in the car, singing about the love of Jesus "down in my heart." I happened to glance at the gas gauge, and to my shock I saw that while we had the love of Jesus in our hearts, we had no gas in our automobile! I must have caught my breath because my wife Nancy turned immediately to me and said, "Rick, you didn't!"

"I did," I said.

She took one look at the gas gauge, then at me, and said "Forget it! We're not going anywhere. Just pull over to the side of the road."

Just then, I saw an exit. The engine died, and the power steering went out. I muscled the car over to the right, and we rolled down the off ramp. There was a yield sign, and no one coming, so we coasted through the sign and across the street, stopping dead still in front of the unleaded pump at the gas station. I never even touched the brakes.

Then I looked over at Nancy and said, "Timed it pretty good, didn't I?"

That's how the Holy Spirit works when we choose the narrow road. He gets us to our destination, even when we've exhausted our own resources. Frequently, that's when He does His best work.

Why choose the narrow road when the broad road seems so much easier? Because the narrow road leads to life. More than once Jesus has healed me and made me well. Maybe He's done the same for you. But I believe He only does so to enable us to *temporarily* labor here on earth. Eventually, I'll be sick again, and so will you.

Maybe it hasn't dawned on you yet, but *none of us are staying here*. But for those who take the narrow road, Jesus Himself will meet us at the end of it, saying, *"Come, you who are blessed of My Father, inherit the kingdom prepared for you from the foundation of the world"* (Matt. 25:34, NASB).

## Wanted: Heroes

We desperately need heroes in our day. Not comic book heroes or movie heroes like Rambo or the Terminator. No, we need real men and women who are heroes of faith to their world. Listen to these words written to Timothy by the apostle Paul, encouraging him to be a hero for Christ Jesus:

> *You, however, continue in the things you have learned and become convinced of, knowing from whom you have learned them; and that from childhood you have known the sacred writings which are able to give you the wisdom that leads to salvation through faith which is in Christ Jesus. All Scripture is inspired by God and profitable for teaching, for reproof, for correction, for training in righteousness; that the man of God may be adequate, equipped for every good work* (2 Tim. 3:14-17, NASB).

When Paul urged Timothy to be a man of integrity, a hero, he pointed him to the Word of God. How can you and I be heroes to our world? By living under the authority of the Bible. This passage says that the Word of God is *inspired*—literally "God-breathed." And because it is God-breathed, it has power in it. When God created the world, He did so with the very breath of His mouth—His voice. What He spoke came into being. When He wanted to communicate with His people in the early days of Israel, He did so through spokesmen, or prophets, who spoke His words, and they carried the weight of His authority. When He wanted to communicate redemp-

tion, the apostle John tells us He did it in the same way
He always had: He spoke the Word.

> *In the beginning was the Word, and the Word
> was with God, and the Word was God. He was in
> the beginning with God. All things came into being
> by Him, and apart from Him nothing came into
> being that has come into being. . . . And the Word
> became flesh, and dwelt among us, and we beheld
> His glory, glory as of the only begotten from the
> Father, full of grace and truth (John 1:1-3;14, NASB).*

God fleshed out His most significant message to us
in the person of Jesus Christ, who came with the full
authority of God Himself. God's Word carries with it
God's authority, period. There are those who argue
that the word "all" in 2 Timothy 3:16 is not literally *all*,
and they seek to define which parts of God's Word are
authoritative and which are not. My literal word for
them is: *baloney!* The Bible is the source of all moral
absolutes—and to toss it aside is to become anchorless,
as many in our world today have come to understand.
The question for the person who wants to be a hero to
their world is this: Do you want to be accepted and
applauded, or do you want to be salt and light to a dying
generation? It is nearly impossible to be both.

My son Joseph received a letter not long ago that I
believe illustrates this. It was sent by Detroit Lions line-
backer Tracy Hayworth, whom I had just met.

> *Dear Joe:*
> *I had the privilege of meeting your father and I am*
> *very grateful. I can't help but think of how great it*
> *must be to have a Dad that cares so much for others*
> *that he goes out of his way to help and teach other*
> *people to understand the meaning of God.*

*As you well know, God is an unpopular subject to most people and they sometimes ridicule anyone that tries to talk to them about it.*

*Let's just face it, people are ready to talk about any and everything until you mention the Bible and then the crowd and friends start to thin out.*

*I am sure you have experienced what I am talking about. It's tough growing up being the son of a reverend! For some reason people either expect different things from you or they expect you to act a certain way.*

*This is hard, but think of how hard it must be for your father to overcome the same obstacles (some a lot more harsh), and still believe and keep his faith and spread it to others who don't even know him or even care.*

*He (your father) has chosen to take a path that not many people travel because of fear and it is too hard to travel. By this, it has made him what everyone in the past, present and future would love to be, a hero. There is one catch. No other hero in the world, whether it be in sports, medicine, the military, etc., can offer a person what your Dad can: a chance of everlasting life. A chance to know Jesus!*

*To me, you have one of the greatest unsung heroes of them all right there at your grasp. Hold on, because he can do you no wrong. Keep the faith.*

*Your friend,*
*Tracy Hayworth, #99*
*Detroit Lions*

During our plane trip, Sparky Anderson asked me, "Rick, what's wrong with the church?" Detroit Tigers pitcher Denny McLain, the last major league pitcher to win over thirty-one games in a season, asked me the same question on another occasion—"What's wrong with the church today?" Moral failures in the church occur for the same reason they occur outside it: we fail to listen to and heed the powerful, true, and authoritative Word of God.

I want to be a man of God. I want to be the kind of man the world can look up to—but to do that, I must obey His Word. If I do, if you do, the world will know immediately that there is something different about us.

## A Hero to My Brothers

Sparky Anderson's words, Denny McLain's words, and Tracy Hayworth's letter to Joseph have served to remind me that I need to be a man of integrity to the world. But I also need to be a man of integrity, a hero, to my brothers and sisters in the faith, "for the sake of those who are chosen," as Paul instructed Timothy. It's tough to be a man of God. The world shoots at you, the culture is against you, Satan battles you, and sometimes you do yourself harm. That's why we need to do all that we can to keep from hurting one another.

Some time back my wife Nancy and I made a commitment that I pray God helps us to keep. We decided we would agree with one another and God never to speak ill against our brothers—no matter what. Our test for what we said about others would not be "Is it true?" but "Is it edifying?" If not, it need not be said. True men of integrity do not tear one another down. They imitate Jesus, who, when He was reviled, reviled not. They imitate His gentleness, His meekness, His self-control. Other men may not know the strength that this kind of commitment requires, but God knows. God knows.

Too often when a Christian man or woman falls or is wounded in some way, the church does not seek to restore them, it seeks to exterminate them! Yet God's Word says *"How good and how pleasant it is for brothers to dwell together in unity!" (Ps. 133:1, NASB)* When one of us is wounded or hurt or fallen, we ought to heal and restore each other—not point out one another's shortcomings. We have the same enemies: the world, the flesh, and the

devil. And we've got the same captain: the Lord Jesus
Christ. We're fellow soldiers and fellow sinners, and
partakers in the same divine and saving grace. When
others are hurt—or when we've been hurt by them— we
establish ourselves as men and women of integrity by
refusing to speak out against our brothers.

I believe this simple act is a part of the "fellowship of
His suffering" that Paul wanted so desperately to experience in his knowledge of Jesus. Not the lashes, not the
thorns, not the nails of the cross—but the lonely suffering
of silence when His words had the power to change
history and condemn His very killers! Part of Jesus' suffering was not opening His mouth against His fellow
men but praying for them and "entrusting Himself to
Him who judges righteously." You and I can trust God
to judge rightly and, eventually, to reward the righteous,
punish the wicked, and make right all that is wrong.
Adding our own commentary, or seeking to do His work,
only damages His kingdom and causes others undue
pain.

## A Hero at Home

For five months in 1993, this preacher did not preach.
I was out of ministry by necessity and spending much-
needed time at home with my family. During this time, I
rediscovered what I already knew: I have a great family.
My wife and our five children are more important to me
than any other people on earth. They know me—and they
love me anyway! I strive every day to know and love
them more. Beth is fifteen. Nancy Jean is fourteen. (Boys
are starting to call and come around, and I'm not sure I
love them, but I'm working on it.) Joseph, my son, is
eleven, and our twins, Mary and Sara, are nine.

When I look at my precious family, I realize that if I
could only be a hero in one arena, I would want to be a
hero at home. If I could be known as a man of integrity
in one place only, I would want that place to be my home.

When I'm out of town preaching, I call home. A lot. Long distance companies love guys like me. I love to hear Nancy's voice when I call just before bedtime and say, "I was wondering, uh, do you . . . ? Do you . . . ? I was wondering . . .", and she says, "Yeah, Rick. I love you. Go to bed now, okay? I love you." I love to hear the kids tell me about their days. I especially love it when I tell Sara, "I love you," and she says with utter assurance, "I know, Daddy." It thrills me that she knows.

It is my heart's conviction that true revival will not come to our land until we Christians start loving one another—and we must begin in our homes, with those we are closest to. Home is where we first learn to love and serve and give. It is where parents model integrity to their children and where a passion for the things of God is "caught."

Last Father's Day I was struggling in my ministry and in my personal battle with addiction, and wondering if I was making a difference anywhere for the Lord. Early in the morning, Nancy Jean left this note on her dad's bed, and when I awoke, I read these words:

> *Dad:*
> *You have done so much for me and you have taught me so much. This Father's Day I wanted to take the time to thank you.*
> *At times I think you are too strict when it comes to friends and boyfriends, but I know it is because you love me. I want you to know that I would never do anything to hurt you. You have taught me to keep my priorities straight and to always put others before myself. You have told me so many times that, though it may be hard, to always love and serve the Lord with all my heart. And you said. . . the best place I will ever be is in His will. You have made so many sacrifices so I could have the best, and when you have given me more than enough, you insist on giving more. You have done your best to keep me in*

*a godly atmosphere, and you have always been a great example. You are so on fire for the Lord and I am trying to be the same way. Just like the song says, "Don't let the fire die."*

*Dad, you will never know how much I look up to you. It is so great to know that no matter how bad I mess up, you will still love me. You have done so much for me, I don't know how to say thank you so I will just say this —Daddy, I love you.*

*Your daughter,*
*Nancy Jean*

Our call is to be people of integrity. To the world. To our brothers and sisters in Christ. To our families. Our call is to be real, authentic people who love Jesus Christ first and best. Canadian physician and author John White has said, "To acknowledge Jesus as Savior and Lord is to join an army. Whether you know it or not, you have enlisted." If you are a Christian, you're in the fight. The world will try to sidetrack us, discredit us, and if possible, distract us. Our job is to be men and women of integrity, determined to make a difference for Him.

An old hymn by Isaac Watts poses this question to those of us who strive for the penny of integrity in a world of choice:

*Am I a soldier of the cross,*
*A follower of the lamb,*
*And shall I fear to own His cause,*
*Or blush to speak His name?*
*In the name, the precious name*
*Of Him who died for me,*
*I'll fight to win the promised crown,*
*Whate'er my cross may be.*

## A Prayer for Integrity

*Dear God, make me a man of integrity. I want to be known in my world, my church, and especially my home as a man who is true to You. God, You are the One I revere above all else. You revealed Yourself to a persecuted slave as El-Roi, the God who sees. I elevate this name above every desire for fame. I lift it up above every wish for pleasure or earthly gain. I declare here and now that the name El-Roi is above every earthly consideration I have now or in the future. How awesome it is to think that You, God, see me. I praise Your name for this.*

*Father, in Your great goodness and the power of Your name, grant to me the power to say no to everything but that which I know is right. Open my eyes that I may see the broad road for the lie that it is. Refresh my spirit once again that I might look with gladness and joy at the narrow road, even when its way is difficult. Please do not let me be detoured by thinking, "No one will notice me here," but give me the sense of Your presence that makes every decision easy in the light of your Holy Love.*

*You, who see me, please open my eyes to clearly see the narrow but lighted path that is before me this day. I ask this for the sake of, and in the name of, the One who went before me Who is Himself the way. . . Jesus my Lord. Amen.*

# Till Death Do Us Part

## The Penny of Devotion

*With this ring, I thee wed,
and stick with you until I'm dead.*
—Rick and Nancy Amato

Statistically, six out of every ten couples who marry in the United States will not remain married for life. Marriage is simply not considered a lifelong undertaking anymore. I read recently that actor Sylvester Stallone's planned marriage to the mother of his three-month-old child is on hold until the two successfully negotiate their prenuptial agreement. He is willing, in the event of their divorce, to give her $1 million a year for each year of marriage up to five, plus $250,000 a year WAM (walking around money) for her and the child. She is holding out for $2 million for each year of marriage, an additional $1 million for having his child, and $1 million a year WAM. Obviously, neither is willing to marry until they can agree on the terms of their divorce!

Relationships today are full of uncertainty. Husbands and wives are unsure that their marriages will last. Children are uncertain that they will grow up with two parents who love one another. The "typical" family that includes a husband, wife, and children conceived by and born to the two of them is anything but typical in the 1990s. It is a rarity. When my wife and I take our kids out to a restaurant and I ask for a table for seven, I get some pretty strange comments and looks. For the record: yes, they are all ours. Beth, Nancy Jean, Joseph, Mary and Sara Amato are our children. We love them and couldn't be more pleased and proud to be the parents of these five fine kids. (I won't go so far as to say we knew exactly what we were doing when we had them—but we're thrilled that God has given them to us to love.)

## A Country in Crisis

There is a crisis in America today. You'd have to be asleep not to know it. Violence is out of control in our cities. Five thousand babies are murdered by abortion in our country every day. Sexually transmitted diseases are increasing at an alarming rate—especially among teenagers. Over 30 million Americans now abuse alcohol. Our prisons are overflowing—and our churches are not. I believe with all my heart that our problems can be traced back to the day when we ceased as a nation to be committed to the family, when we abandoned God's principles of commitment and purpose and surrendered to the flow of a culture that is growing sicker and sicker each and every day.

It was not always this way. God did not intend for it to be so. He had a tremendous design for abundant living—and His Son Jesus Christ proclaimed that fact when he came to redeem mankind: *"I am the door;"* He said, *"if anyone enters through Me, he shall be saved, and shall go in and out, and find pasture. The thief comes only to steal, and kill, and destroy. I came that they might have life, and might have it abundantly"* (*John 10:9-10, NASB*).

No nation on the face of the earth is big enough or powerful enough to shake its fist in the face of God and prosper. And although we are still a nation that professes belief in God (95 percent of Americans believe in God, according to a recent survey by *U.S. News and World Report*), we have abandoned His principles in our everyday lives and especially in our families. Sixty percent of Americans say they attend church regularly and there are certainly plenty of churches to attend. The United States has more churches than any nation on earth—one to every 900 people. But we are ill-equipped to live out our belief in a multicultural, postmodernist society.

So what do we do? Do we blame our president? (I can't—these problems began long before he took office.) Do we blame the Senate, or the House of Representatives, or the educational system, or the neighbors? Or do we look soberly at our own lives and understand that there will be no changes in Washington, or anywhere else for that matter, until there is a change in our homes? No builder begins without a blueprint, and to build solid, God-honoring homes and relationships, we need a plan. I am grateful God has provided one.

## The First Couple, by Design

The account of creation in Genesis tells us that God was pleased with every aspect of His marvelous handiwork. There was light and God saw that it was good. Heavens, the earth, and waters—and He saw that it was good. Plants, fruit trees, and all kinds of vegetation—and God called it good. The sun and moon and stars to light the night sky were all deemed good in God's sight. Only once in this account does God say that something is not good. *"Then the LORD God said, 'It is not good for the man to be alone; I will make him a helper suitable for him'"(Gen. 2:18, NASB).*

Anyone who questions whether the Lord God has a sense of humor needs to carefully study what follows this proclamation in Genesis, chapter two. A virtual "parade" of created life-forms marches before the man Adam, and he finds no "helper suitable for him" from their number. Imagine Adam examining a gorilla. "It's very nice," he must have thought. "And I am lonely—but not that lonely." Or picture him wondering if perhaps a duck would be a suitable helpmeet, then saying (in Hebrew, of course), "Uh-uh." Not one suitable helper for Adam was found among all of the animals God created. So God tailor-made one.

> *"So the* LORD *God caused a deep sleep to fall upon the man, and he slept; then He took one of his ribs, and closed up the flesh at that place. And the* LORD *God fashioned into a woman the rib which He had taken from the man, and brought her to the man" (Gen. 2:21-22,* NASB).

Then an amazing thing happened. Adam recognized immediately that God had perfectly met his need in this newly-created woman. He said "This! This is it! Bone of my bones and flesh of my flesh!" She was a perfect companion for him, and something in his spirit confirmed it.

## *"I'm Going to Marry That Girl"*

I saw my wife Nancy for the first time when I was seventeen years old. My buddy Norman Maurer and I had walked into church together the evening she was to be baptized, and when I saw her, my soul did a flip-flop. She was standing with a long-haired boy (whom I later discovered was her boyfriend), and I punched Norman in the side and said these words: "Norman—you see that girl there? I'm going to marry that girl someday." I was seventeen and full of fire for the Lord (and, I confess, for girls as well), but I wasn't the kind of person who said that about every pretty girl I spotted. I think somehow I felt what Adam must have felt when he first laid eyes on his God-given helpmeet: "This is it!"

I managed to catch her as she was going out the door, and asked the boy she was with, "Are you saved?" He said he wasn't. He believed in God, he told me, but wasn't ready to stop running from Him yet. I looked him dead in the eye and said, "Well, if you're not careful, He's going to call you home and somebody else is going to get your girl."

Somebody did. Nancy and I became sweethearts and we have been together ever since. When I left her in Detroit to attend Liberty University in Virginia, I discovered that being away from her was unbearable. I would drive seventeen hours to spend two hours with her, then turn around and drive seventeen more back to school. I took the three hundred dollars I had been given for food that summer and bought her an engagement ring. Then I ate tuna fish and crackers for months with no regrets.

We were so young. I know looking back that the odds were certainly against our making it. Although we were both saved, we made many mistakes. Our physical involvement before marriage was not God-honoring, and that is something we both regret deeply to this day. I was brash and immature and was just learning to be a man. But we had one very important thing in our favor: we both knew our union was for keeps. Neither of us thought for a moment that our commitment was anything less than total. It was for life. We said, "Till death do us part," and we meant it. Even today, we look at each other sometimes and say what we said often in those early days: "With this ring, I thee wed, and stick with you until I'm dead."

As far as I was concerned, God had done for me what He did for Adam: He had made a helper for me and brought her to me. She was and is my companion. That is still His plan for husbands and wives: one man with one woman for life. Companions until death do you part. Nancy and I are devoted to one another, to our marriage, and to our children until one or both of us dies. Period. There have been times when quitting certainly would have been easier than working through our problems together, but I thank God we never considered that to be an option.

I believe God is angry with America because of the way many of her men have treated their God-given companions. He had a similar complaint years ago against the nation of Judah:

> *Judah has dealt treacherously, and an abomination has been committed in Israel and in Jerusalem; for Judah has profaned the sanctuary of the LORD which He loves, and has married the daughter of a foreign god. As for the man who does this, may the LORD cut off from the tents of Jacob everyone who awakes and answers, or who presents an offering to the LORD of hosts. And this is another thing you do: you cover the altar of the LORD with tears, with weeping and with groaning, because He no longer regards the offering or accepts it with favor from your hand. Yet you say, "For what reason?" Because the LORD has been a witness between you and the wife of your youth, against whom you have dealt treacherously, though she is your companion, and your wife by covenant (Mal. 2:11-14, NASB).*

The men of Judah were not devoted to the women God gave them as companions, and He held them accountable for their lack of commitment. Their offerings did not please Him, and all their weeping, groaning and tears did nothing to change that fact. A great deal of what is wrong with America (and with the church) is that we men have forgotten how absolutely important our wives are. A man and his companion are God's priority on earth—and we have failed to recognize that.

## Words from the Rule Book

If God intends marriage to prosper, what instructions does He give to insure its health? Very simply, He gives one key command to husbands and another key command to wives. To husbands, God says, *"Love your wives, just as Christ also loved the church and gave Himself up for her" (Eph. 5:25, NASB).* Husbands are commanded to love their wives—as Christ loved the church and as they love their own bodies. To love your wife as you love your own body means to do for her what you do for yourself. To look out for her the way you look out for yourself. To consider her welfare the way you consider your own. How would you feel if someone didn't rinse out the tub after taking a shower—for fourteen years? How would you feel if, when the trash can is full, someone mashed down one more piece of trash, or balanced something else precariously on the top of the heap instead of carrying it out? Husbands, love your wives—and demonstrate your love by caring for her in a sacrificial way.

What about wives? God's command to them is equally straightforward: *"Wives, be subject to your own husbands, as to the Lord. For the husband is the head of the wife, as Christ also is the head of the church" (Eph. 5:22-23, NASB).* I was preaching recently in Colorado and received a message that my wife was on the phone and had an urgent question. I listened to her, then said "Okay honey, that sounds great. You go right ahead. I love you too. Bye." Someone nearby asked if everything was all right, and I said that it was. I explained that Nancy just wanted to know if it was okay to take all the kids out for lunch on Sunday.

I could tell by the looks I got that some of the bystanders were wondering if I was some kind of domestic dictator and my wife was a doormat. I'm not. She's not either. If you knew Nancy, you'd know that. Nancy is a strong, strong woman. She has one speed: fast. She has one tone: loud. She's determined, competent, and self-assured. But in my home, we have a budget. I set aside funds for outside meals and entertainment, and Nancy polices those expenditures. There was a question as to whether or not we would go beyond what we'd set aside, and she left the last word to me.

Our home follows the biblical chain of command. Christ is the head of the church, and the husband is the head of the wife. In most matters, we have little or no trouble reaching agreement. But when we do not agree, I have the responsibility of making the call. Nancy is her own woman, with her own strong identity in Christ. She nurtures her relationship with Him, as well as our relationship. Submitting to her husband does not mean becoming a nonthinking person. We are equally important in our marriage, and we are joint heirs in Jesus Christ, but our roles are different!

God designed marriage to reflect His glory and to be a living, breathing picture of His relationship to His bride, the church. When husbands fulfill their God-ordained role in the home, and wives do likewise, abundant living—"life in excess"— is manifested. Nancy is devoted to me, and I am devoted to her. In all the ups and downs of our life together (and there have been many), she has been there.

A few years into our marriage, I was preaching a service at Thomas Road Baptist Church in Virginia. I did not know it, but Jerry Falwell Jr. had invited former Pittsburgh Steeler quarterback Terry Bradshaw to attend. At the close of the service, I gave the invitation, and one man stepped out and came forward, followed by nearly half of the congregation. As I took his hand, he said "Please pray for me." I asked him his name, and he said, "Terry Bradshaw." I said, "*the* Terry Bradshaw?" He said, "That's right."

I prayed for him right there, and as he turned to go, hundreds followed him. I thought I had preached the sermon of my life, but they had come forward to see this sports superstar. Then Nancy stepped up to my side from the front row, and I said, "Nancy— did you see that? Did you see who came forward and asked me to pray for him?" She leveled her gaze at me and said calmly, "No, Rick. But I saw that the dog came forward at home and dragged trash all over the yard—and you need to pick it up when you get there." Nancy has been the one who is always there after the crowds are gone. Sometimes with a humbling word, sometimes with comfort, sometimes with a challenge. But she is always there.

## A Picture of Devotion

My marriage has not been without uncertain times. I have faced life-threatening illness and dealt with serious drug addiction. We have been evicted, and we have had our car repossessed. We lived with my sister, Peggy, who took us in when we had nothing. No home, no car, no money. Nothing. My kids remember seven of us living in a house with no heat and broken out windows, and Detroit winters can get cold—sometimes down to thirty below zero. We didn't have food, but it didn't matter because we didn't have a refrigerator to put it in. I went through a period when I was in total rebellion against God, and that did not make me a pleasant person to live with. My daughter Beth Ann says she used to pray on her knees at night, "God, please don't let Mommy and Daddy hurt each other." Nancy Jean would cry when she heard us shout at one another, and Beth would hold her and try to comfort her.

But if you asked Nancy if she ever considered divorce, she would tell you no. My wife is not a quitter, thank God. Her devotion amazes and humbles me. When we were financially broken, she trusted God to provide, and He did. When she was forced to deal with the Jekyll-and-Hyde personality of an addict in denial, she persevered. To this day I cannot understand from a human perspective why my wife stayed with me.

Have we had our share of hard times? Yes. Do we fight? Yes, we do. Are we still together? Yes. And are we more in love than ever? Yes, we are. Devotion is a commitment to meet the needs of another person through the power of the Holy Spirit, and my wife and I are devoted to one another.

I can't begin to count how many times in the last seventeen years I have picked up the phone to call Nancy and found her on the other end of the line before I had a chance to start dialing. Or how often the phone rings and I hear her voice, just as I was about to call her. Hundreds of times, I know. We are somehow "in tune" to one another—and that to me is evidence of the "one flesh" aspect of marriage. Just as many times, I'm sure, we have turned to one another and said the same words at the same time. People even tell us we are beginning to look alike. (Pray for my wife!) When a man and woman are truly devoted to one another and committed to their marriage, they can't pursue others, flirt, or entertain for even a moment the advances of a member of the opposite sex, but they're not missing anything. Because when you are committed to your mate, the two of you can get so close that God whispers into your ears at the same time, and you hear His voice as one!

One of the decisions Nancy and I made early in our marriage has paid off richly in the years since. The number one reason marriages fail is adultery. Knowing that, we erected a "hedge" around our marriage by agreeing with one another never to be alone with a member of the opposite sex. Do you think avoiding such situations is impossible? It's not! By God's grace we have both kept that promise, and by His grace it has kept us. My vocation means that we are separated more than either of us would like, and there have been times that it has been inconvenient to hold to our agreement, but I have.

I was in Los Angeles some time back, scheduled to appear on a television program. I was staying at the Beverly Hills Hilton, and received a call from the desk saying, "Reverend Amato, your ride to the television station is here." I walked downstairs and out the door, and the bellman directed me to a very attractive blond woman in a cute red convertible. She pulled up to the curb, smiled, and said "I'm your ride." I smiled right back and said, "No, you're not." Then I explained that I could not get in the car with her, and I'm sure she thought I was crazy. (After all, this was California!) I turned to go back to my room, talking to myself the whole way. "You blew it," I said. "Now you'll never get God's message out to the people who would have seen that show."

A short time after I returned upstairs, the phone rang again. "Reverend Amato," the voice said, "your ride is here." I was dumbfounded. I went downstairs again and saw the same red convertible, only this time, there were two people inside. As the blond pulled up again, she said, "Hi. This is the station manager. Climb in." And we made it to the interview with minutes to spare.

Husbands, are you serious about safeguarding your marriage? Wives, are you? Husbands, is your wife growing in the Lord? Are you doing all that you can to see that she is becoming the woman God intended her to be? Is your marriage worth that effort?

## *Children Are God's Gift*

*"Children are a gift of the LORD,"* wrote King Solomon. *"The fruit of the womb is a reward. Like arrows in the hand of a warrior, so are the children of one's youth. How blessed is the man whose quiver is full of them"* (Ps. 127:3-5, NASB). I grew up in a dysfunctional family, as one of seven children. I am still discovering how my childhood has affected my own family and my feelings about fatherhood. But I did have a very loving and caring and affectionate Italian father. God was not exalted in the home of my youth. He wasn't lifted up and praised. Prayer was not a priority. Jesus wasn't first, and Daddy wasn't second, but that's changed in my home. Jesus is the boss today, Mommy and Daddy work together, and Daddy has the final say. We do it that way because that's God's way and because it works—and we're having a riot!

Solomon was right about the man with many children (a quiver full) being a happy man. Our five children have brought me more happiness than I deserve and more than I ever dreamed I would know. Beth, our oldest, is a cheerleader, a basketball player, a student council officer, and a comedienne. She ministers laughter to us, and when she is "on a roll," we laugh until our sides ache. Nancy Jean is our most intensely spiritual child. We are not surprised when we open a closet to see Nancy Jean, face to the floor, praying. She is up early seeking God. It's not unusual to see her reading her Bible late into the night. She traveled to Russia with me when she was only eleven—and was the first American child ever to speak in the Kremlin.

Joseph, our son, is the fireball of the family. He never stops. When I put him to bed at night, he's never tired. "Dad, I gotta run, I gotta play—there's baseball, Dad, and . . ." Then he's out. Like a light. He's a long ball hitter with a tender heart and a mind for mischief—and he's our boy.

Mary and Sara are our twins. They live together. They each have their own bed, but when you go into their bedroom in the morning, they're sleeping crammed into the same one. Mary's my prayer warrior. She prays the most impossible prayers, and while we're snickering at her naive innocence, God is answering them! Sara is the quiet one. She's always sucking her thumb and watching everything. She's a fun lover with a sweet, sweet heart.

When my health became a serious issue just a few years ago, God showed me the importance of being a father to my children. I literally thought that I was dying, and as Nancy drove me to the hospital, I was saying hysterical things like, "Don't give anyone my fishing poles, I don't want someone else using them," and "Be careful how you spend the insurance money," and "Don't marry some other old man and bring him into our house." When I was situated in my room and waiting to see the doctor, I began to think more clearly—and what God brought to mind was this: "Rick, you've preached in Russia, and you've preached in Cuba, and you've traveled all over the world with the gospel. Now who will teach your children? Who will teach Nancy Jean and Beth? Who will introduce Joseph and Mary and Sara to Jesus? Who, Rick?"

I decided then and there that if I lived, I was going to become a different kind of dad. And I have. My children say I'm not the way I was before. You can fool a lot of folks, but you can seldom fool children—especially your own. I came home from the hospital and began to get my priorities right. We received wise counsel as a family and faced some old "demons" together for the first time. Since then, the income of Rick Amato Ministries has dropped nearly $1 million. Out of hundreds of invitations to preach, I've accepted less than twenty in the past year. I had forgotten my children, but now they are my joy, and they know it.

Children are a gift from God, but raising them is a challenge! Number one, they eat a lot! They make a huge mess. They don't like to go to sleep, and they don't like to wake up (except on Christmas morning). But what you and I invest in the lives of our children will last. The man who lives to impress his coworkers or his friends, or to gain the world's applause, will die a pauper. It's true. Oh, they'll gather to pay their respects, and a few will even eulogize him with kind words. A minister will pray over him, and people will say he'll be missed. But they'll put him in the ground and shovel dirt over his grave— and life will go on much the same as it did before. But the man who pours life and love and sacrificial giving into his family leaves memories and lessons implanted in their hearts that will never die.

## "Let Me See Your Glory, God"

Years ago in college I read the story of how Joshua prayed, "Lord, show me Your glory." And God showed His glory to Joshua. Then I read how Moses prayed in the same way, "God, show me Your glory," and Moses saw the glory of God. The goal of my life then, as it is now, was to know God—and I, too, wanted to see His glory. So my friend Daniel Henderson and I agreed to fast and pray for 21 days that we might see the glory of God. I thought perhaps I would see some supernatural vision or hear a word from Him through a great pastor or teacher that was intended just for me. But at the end of our three-week fast, I had seen nothing.

On the twenty-second day, I came home from school very late in the evening, and my house was quiet. I walked in the door and down the hall, and I could hear my children breathing quietly in their beds. Have you ever listened to sleeping children breathe? Isn't it a beautiful sound? I went to Joseph's bed and placed my face next to his. "Jesus is Lord," I whispered, and as he has so many times before, he sighed and nodded slightly at the sound of my voice. I tiptoed down the hall and into Beth and Nancy Jean's room and, kneeling between them, whispered, "You're going to be women of God." All three children were showered and shampooed, and their hair had been perfectly combed. They looked angelic to me.

I walked past the bathroom, and looking in, I noticed that the toilet was gleaming! Three children and one adult had cleaned themselves up in our one tiny bathroom earlier that night, but it was spotless. No towels on the floor. No water standing. I thought of how many times I had been proud to bring my friends and college professors to our little home on Stratford Road. We didn't have much furniture, but it was the cleanest house in Virginia!

When I opened the door to our bedroom, I saw Nancy sound asleep in a blue nightgown, with one leg off the bed. I knew she was totally exhausted. And I thought about the struggles she had experienced with her health and the emotional abuse she withstood at times from the evil man inside me. I thought of how she loved me in spite of myself and how she had maintained her identity and personality, even after seven years with a stubborn, Italian preacher.

Then I saw it. There in my own bedroom I saw the Shekinah glory of God resting on His sleepy but satisfied homemaker. He showed Himself to me, not through a powerful vision or the burning words of some modern-day prophet, but through the everyday grace of an ordered home and a devoted wife, struggling to put her rebellious husband through college. I understood then what I am telling you now: It's not a disgrace to be a submissive wife—it's an honor. It's not a shame to be a crying, loving, hugging husband and father—it's a privilege, and it's the greatest strength that God can give a man. A devoted companion and children are priceless blessings from the Lord. Pennies of purest joy from His hand. Happy is the man whose "pockets" are full with them. I know.

## A Prayer for Devotion

Yahweh Shamma, *the God who is there, we praise and revere your name.*

*Please make us faithful men and women, as You are faithful to Your own. You said You would betroth your people to You forever "in righteousness and justice, in loving-kindness and in compassion and in faithfulness." We know so little of that kind of devotion, but God, teach us more! Help us to honor and cherish the companions you have given to us as husbands and wives and to consider our children above work or any other worldly distraction that we might mistakenly place above them.*

*Bring a revival to our land, Father, beginning in our homes. Let us be alert to the snares the enemy might set to destroy marriages that honor You. Make us willing to go to any lengths to protect the sacred bond that exists between a husband and a wife. Remind us when the way is hard that we promised to our mates not to quit, and help us to keep that promise regardless of the cost.*

*Oh, God of Abraham, Isaac, and Jacob, may we build into our families a godly heritage and a passion to know You. Nothing else is so important as that. Make us devoted lovers of our mates, devoted parents to our children, and devoted soldiers of the cross of Your Son and our Savior, Jesus Christ, for that is abundant life. Amen.*

# Learning to Wait
## The Penny of Patience

*Second only to suffering, waiting may be the greatest teacher and trainer in godliness, maturity, and genuine spirituality most of us ever encounter.*
—Richard Hendrix

Once there was a time when people waited for ordinary things. They waited for their dinner to cook on the kitchen stove or in the oven. (There were no microwaves.) They waited to speak with people who were already talking on the telephone. (There was no Call Waiting.) They waited for the mail and the daily newspaper. (There were no faxes or car phones, no E-mail, voice mail, videocams, or satellite uplinks.) Once children even waited for their parents to call them home for dinner. (There were no electronic pagers.) But waiting is becoming a lost art in today's high tech communication bonanza. No one chooses to wait anymore when there are so many convenient alternatives.

Waiting may be my least favorite activity under the sun. I'm Italian—and impatient—so I hate to wait. When Rick Amato Ministries was at the height of its involvement in Russia in 1991, some business consultants advised that we stop all our activities for three months to develop a five-year action plan. I thought it was the most unreasonable suggestion I had ever heard. There was so much to be done! So I disregarded their advice and pressed on until finally, I burned out. Then I found myself in a Rapha psychiatric unit facing a recurring problem with addictive behavior and a dependence on prescription drugs. Imagine my frustration when my Rapha counselors strongly suggested that I do nothing for three months, giving myself time to heal. I was so sick I had little choice. This time I waited.

What I feared would happen if I stood still, did. We teetered on the brink of financial disaster. Our ministry's income was dependent on me being on the road, and I was home, resting. I knew I needed to get well—but I also knew I needed to be responsible for myself, my family, and my RAM employees. Our accounts payable skyrocketed. We owed over $35,000, including a final payment for the printing of Russian Bibles, and for the first time in our history, we did not have the operating funds to cover our rent. I began moving furniture out of the office and into our garage, and prepared Nancy, the kids, and our staff for the worst.

I was using a devotional book during that time called *Streams in the Desert*. One morning I read about Moses' experience on the edge of the Red Sea, with the Egyptian army closing in fast. God told him the strangest thing in this desperate circumstance! "Stand still," He said, "and see the salvation of the Lord." Imagine! *Stand still*. The message spoke profoundly to my heart, and I wondered if Moses must have felt as I did—trapped between specific instructions to do nothing and an intense desire to do something—anything!

The next Sunday morning in worship my pastor, Dr. Lloyd Locklear, stood and said, "Today I'm going to preach from Isaiah, chapter 40, verse 31. *'Those who wait for the LORD Will gain new strength; They will mount up with wings like eagles, They will run and not get tired, they will walk and not become weary,'" (NASB)*. My daughter Nancy Jean had given me the same verse just a short time before. I listened carefully. Then that Sunday night, Pastor Locklear walked to the pulpit and said, "God has led me to preach tonight from Exodus, chapter 14," and the hair on the back of my neck stood up. I sat straighter as I heard him read the words of Moses that had captured my heart days before:

*"'Do not be afraid! Stand still by and see the salvation of the LORD, which He will accomplish for you today. For the Egyptians whom you see today, you shall see again no more forever. The LORD will fight for you, and you shall hold hold your peace'" (Ex. 14:13-14, NASB).*

I could not get home fast enough when the service had ended. I went into my study, opened my Bible to the same text, and began to dig deep into the meaning of the words. The situation described was certainly a no-win. The Red Sea stood before Moses and the sons of Israel, and the Egyptian army marched at their heels. Moses' credibility as a man of God was on the line as never before. Logic demanded that he take a high dive into the sea and hope for the best, or rally the troops for one last battle with the mighty warriors of Egypt. But logic is not the sole consideration in any crisis. With Yahweh, there is always another option. It lies not in front of you, or behind you, but above you.

The voice that spoke to Moses said, "Stand still and see the salvation of the LORD." When I looked up those same words in the Hebrew, I was shocked to find that their literal meaning had been God's message to me time and time again. "Stand still" was *yawstab*, meaning to position oneself to be still. Not just to cease moving, but to get into a position where stillness could manifest itself. "And see" was *rawaw*—to behold something with wide-eyed awe and amazement. I experienced *rawaw* the first time I saw the crown jewels of Russia in the marble-lined maze beneath the Kremlin in Moscow. I stood as close to the tiara of Princess Elizabeth as I possibly could, leaning into the glass with my jaw slack and my eyes wide. "Rick," the guides called, "Rick, we are going now." But I couldn't tear my gaze away from the tiara's beauty. That's *rawaw*. The third word was *yeshua*—and it means

Jesus. Jesus is "the salvation of the LORD." So the command, "Stand still and see the salvation of the LORD" is *yawstab rawaw yeshua*, or "Get still, and get close to Jesus." Isn't that wonderful advice for any man or woman who must wait?

Moses needed to get still and get close to his deliverer. I needed that in the spring of '93—and I need it just as much today. My life has been full of experience after experience in which I chose to fight on my own strength or flee rather than wait on God. Every time I have jumped out ahead of Him, I have landed in the desert or in a prison of some kind—even a few of my own making! Every time. The lesson He has tried to teach me again and again is to wait on Him. *"I waited patiently for the LORD,"* David wrote in *Psalm 40, "and He inclined to me, and heard my cry" (v.1, NASB)*. The word David used for *waited* has double emphasis in the Hebrew. It says literally, "in waiting, I waited."

Most of us know so little of waiting. We bargain, promote, push, scheme, and deal our way through life. We'll do anything rather than wait. Yet God's desire for us is that we learn to trust in His Word and be patient for its manifestation in our lives. How many of us could say as David did, "My soul waits in silence for God only"? Too few, I'm afraid. When we are forced to wait, we try not to do it in silence. Muzak is supplied to fill the silence of a short elevator ride. Sales messages and more Muzak fill the silence of being put on hold. I'm told you can even purchase tapes of "nature sounds" like the sea or a thunderstorm to fill the silence in your home or to help you fall asleep! But Jesus welcomed the periods of silence and solitude He was able to build into His ministry-filled days. His time alone with God fed Him and equipped Him.

## Trading Stress for Rest

Our impatience produces stress, but the virtue of patience produces rest. The world will work us to death if we let it, but Jesus gives rest. He even promised rest in His invitation to would-be disciples: *"Come to Me, all who are weary and heavy-laden, and I will give you rest. Take My yoke upon you, and learn from Me, for I am gentle and humble in heart; and YOU SHALL FIND REST FOR YOUR SOULS"* (Matt. 11:28-29, NASB). God does not intend for Christians to live their lives in a frantic, frazzled, desperate sprint. Over and over in Scripture, the principles of patient waiting and rest appear—and the lives of many men of God were marked by their ability or inability to wait.

## Where's a Prophet When You Need One?

Israel's first king was not a man of patience. King Saul began to reign at age forty, anointed by the prophet Samuel. God's plan was to speak through Samuel to Saul regarding the nation of Israel, but that arrangement was not pleasing to Saul for long! After his anointing, Samuel sent the king to Gilgal with these instructions: *"And you shall go down before me to Gilgal; and behold, I will come down to you to offer burnt offerings and sacrifice peace offerings. You shall wait seven days until I come to you and show you what you should do"* (1 Sam. 10:8, NASB).

Saul did go to Gilgal as Samuel instructed, but circumstances made it difficult for the impetuous king to wait for further instruction from God's prophet. After Saul's son Jonathan defeated a garrison of Philistine warriors in nearby Gibean, the Philistines amassed an army of horsemen and chariots and prepared to attack the Israelites in revenge. The men of Israel were so frightened they hid in caves, cliffs, and holes in the ground. The king managed to wait in Gilgal for seven days in the face of this terrible threat, but when Samuel did not come, the people began to scatter. What was a king to do? Where was a prophet when you needed one?

Instead of waiting, Saul decided to do Samuel's job for him. *"So Saul said, 'Bring to me the burnt offering and the peace offerings.' And he offered the burnt offering. And it came* about as soon as he finished offering the burnt offering, that behold, Samuel came; and Saul went out to meet him and to greet him" (1 Sam. 13:9-10, NASB). Samuel asked Saul what he had done, and Saul was ready with excuses:

> *Because I saw that the people were scattering from me, and that you did not come within the appointed days, and that the Philistines were assembling at Michmash, therefore I said, "Now the Philistines will come down against me at Gilgal, and I have not asked the favor of the LORD." So I forced myself and offered the burnt offering* (1 Sam. 13:11-12, NASB).

Saul told Samuel that he "forced himself" to act. Could he not have "forced himself" to wait? Or did he think waiting was not an action suited to a king and military leader? Waiting takes tremendous faith and shows a true depth of character. It is hard to wait. But the consequences of failing to do so can be life-changing. Saul's royal dynasty ended the day he superseded God's command through Samuel. David's ascension to the throne was insured the day Saul ceased to wait on God. "'But now your kingdom shall not endure,'" said Samuel. "'The LORD has sought out for Himself a man after His own heart, and the LORD has appointed him as ruler over His people, because you have not kept what the LORD commanded you'" (1 Sam. 13:14, NASB).

Saul was like so many of us who allow ourselves to become captives of circumstance. He was more afraid to wait than he was to disobey! It's true that Samuel was late. It's true that a huge army was staring the Israelites square in the face. It's true that his soldiers and subjects were looking to him for some kind of response. But those facts were no truer than God's promises and His commands. Saul put himself and the Israelites in more danger by his refusal to wait than they faced from any Philistine army, and so do we when we cease to wait on Him.

## Toes Sticking Out of the Sand

Moses too learned a powerful lesson in patience before God called him to deliver the nation of Israel from its slavery in Egypt. Raised in the palace by the daughter of Pharaoh, Moses was treated as an Egyptian prince from infancy. When he became a man, he understood that he was a Hebrew by birth—and one day as he watched an Egyptian beating one of his Hebrew brothers, it became too much for him to bear. When he was sure that no one was looking, he killed the offending Egyptian and buried him in the sand.

Sure that his sin was buried and probably pleased that he had acted on Israel's behalf, Moses went out the next day and saw two Hebrews fighting with one another. When he stopped to intervene, one of them shocked him with these words: "'Who made you a prince or a judge over us? Are you intending to kill me, as you killed the Egyptian?'" (Ex. 2:14, NASB) He was found out! He had buried the Egyptian he murdered, but his secret did not stay buried. Toes sticking out of the sand told the story. When Pharaoh heard what Moses had done, he tried to kill him, but Moses fled to a land called Midian to hide out there. As a result of his impetuousness, he spent years on the back side of nowhere before he was finally commissioned by God to do the very task he attempted on his own once before!

As a prince, Moses must have felt equipped to lead the Hebrews out of their oppression, but years of quiet living as a Midian shepherd took some of the brashness from his character. He learned to wait in Midian. When God did call him to be a deliverer, his response was tempered quite a bit from those early years: "'Who am I, that I should go to Pharaoh, and that I should bring the sons of Israel out of Egypt?'" (Ex. 3:11, NASB) God promised Moses His presence, and Moses led the Hebrews out, looking to God for direction at each turn.

I identify with Moses. My impetuousness and my temper have gotten me into trouble too. I have spoken dreams when I should have kept silent, and acted rashly when I should have waited patiently on God to lead. I have felt like I was tending sheep on the back side of nowhere, and I have chafed to be "where the action was" when all in my world was quiet. But when I have waited on God and obeyed Him, it has always been worth the wait. Charles Spurgeon wrote, "Remember, the longer the blessing is coming, the richer it will be when it arrives. That which is gained speedily by a single prayer is sometimes only a second-rate blessing; but that which is gained after many a desperate tug and many an awful struggle is a full-weighted and precious blessing."[1] Waiting is a penny from God, the flip-side of which is patience and whose blessing is only fully understood with time.

## Don't Miss God's Rest

One of the warnings the writer of Hebrews issued to his readers was not to miss God's rest: *"Therefore, let us fear lest, while a promise remains of entering His rest, any one of you should seem to have come short of it"* (Heb. 4:1, NASB). There is a rest that is unique to believers, and we should strive for it—not for quotas or accolades or awards from men. If you or I don't have rest, we are not with Jesus, because rest is what He gives! When we work in our own power, our own strength, our own might, we cease to rest in Jesus.

I don't know a single person who doesn't wish for more time. Most of us have an unwritten (but vaguely haunting) list of things we never got done. Letters we didn't write, places we didn't visit, books we didn't read, words we didn't speak, etc. I was addicted to drugs at one point in my life—and that may have never happened to you—but most people I know are addicted to motion and suffer from what I call *time sickness*. The symptoms of time sickness are easy to identify: constant motion, rushing, things done hurriedly, things left undone, and the inability to focus on one thing at a time. Those who suffer from time sickness are too worried about what they need to do next to sit quietly for even sixty seconds! They've got things to do, people to see, places to go—and so they've got to keep moving.

Ministers can be especially vulnerable to time sickness. Greater experience in ministry brings more and more assignments until we find ourselves doing more "for God," but enjoying Him less. In truth, our problem is not one of time, it's one of perspective. We have substituted what is urgent for what is important, and we need an eternal perspective in order to understand what really matters. Jesus said as much to Martha, the overzealous hostess and sister of Lazarus and Mary in Luke's Gospel. After Martha welcomed Jesus into their home, Mary stationed herself at Jesus' feet and listened with rapt attention to His teaching. Martha, on the other hand, paid little attention to the teacher but busied herself with food preparation and other details.

When Mary never managed to tear herself away and help her busy sister, Martha protested to Jesus Himself: *"Lord, do You not care that my sister has left me to do all the serving alone? Then tell her to help me."* Jesus' answer must have stunned her: *"Martha, Martha, you are worried and bothered about so many things; but only a few things are necessary, really only one, for Mary has chosen the good part, which shall not be taken away from her"* (Luke 10:40-42, NASB). Patience produces rest. Impatience produces stress. Mary patiently listened at the feet of Jesus and was totally at rest. Her sister impatiently threw a meal together without help and felt no joy at all in the presence of her guest—only stress.

Jesus is the perfect picture of a man completely at rest in God. He was able, at His death, to say, "I have finished the work You set out for Me to do," but He had not healed all the sick, saved all the lost, freed all the captives, or given sight to all the blind. What had He done? All that the Father commanded—and only what the Father commanded. Time never ruled Jesus Christ—He ruled over it! When His family, the disciples, or the multitudes tried to hurry Him, He refused to be pressed. They thought a lap full of children might be an imposition. He quickly let them know the little ones were a priority. They thought the imminent death of His close friend Lazarus was a crisis demanding immediate attention. He saw it instead as an opportunity to wait for God's glory to be manifested. There would be no opportunity in healing a man of the flu (or whatever ailment Lazarus suffered from) to declare, "I am the resurrection and the life. He who believes in Me shall live, even though he dies." To raise His friend Lazarus from the dead required that He wait when the whole world said, "Go!"

## Transformed by Waiting

Who you and I become while we wait is more important than whatever we are waiting for. Through the penny of patience, God transforms our character. Abram waited for the promises of God and became Abraham, the father of nations. His is the first name listed in Matthew's genealogy of Jesus Christ, "the son of David, the son of Abraham" (*Matt. 1:1, NASB*). Sarai waited for the promises too, and in the process she became Sarah, mother of Isaac. Joseph became the number two man in all of Egypt—second only to Pharaoh—after waiting years in prison for a crime he did not commit. When he was released at age thirty, he had acquired the mature faith that enabled him to reconcile with his family and save them from starving to death in Canaan.

Abraham, Sarah, Joseph, and countless others discovered that waiting patiently for the promises of God transformed their very lives, just as it will transform ours if we allow it to do so. The trick is to see waiting not as a trial to be endured, but as a process God uses to make us into the people He created us to be. The very fact that I am a

Christian means that I am waiting for the return of my Savior, Jesus Christ! The apostle Paul described it this way:

> *"For we know that the whole creation groans and suffers the pains of childbirth together until now. And not only this, but also we ourselves, having the first fruits of the Spirit, even we ourselves groan within ourselves, waiting eagerly for our adoption as sons, the redemption of our body. For in hope we have been saved, but hope that is seen is not hope; for why does one also hope for what he sees? But if we hope for what we do not see, with perseverance we wait eagerly for it"* (Rom. 8:22-25, NASB).

And as we do, we are changed.

## A God Who Waits

While we are waiting people only by necessity—our God is a waiting God by choice! Simon Peter wrote:

> *"But do not let this one fact escape your notice, beloved, that with the Lord one day is as a thousand years, and a thousand years as one day. The Lord is not slow about His promise, as some count slowness, but is patient toward you, not wishing for any to perish but for all to come to repentance"* (2 Pet. 3:8-9, NASB).

Isn't that amazing? The God of the universe waited for you and waited for me—and He is still waiting patiently (even though our world deserves His judgment) for others to turn to Him.

Possibly the most vivid picture in all of the Bible of God's waiting is found in Jesus' account of the prodigal son, recorded in the Gospel of Luke. The prodigal son is you and me—gone the way of the world and totally detached from his loving father. The father, of course, is God, waiting each day with the hope that his wayward son will return. How he must have scanned the horizon every evening, wondering, "Will he come tonight?" He never ceased to wait. But when the day came that his son made the first tentative steps back to his home and his family, on that day, the father could wait no more. When he saw his son coming a long way in the distance, he ran!

We think when we wait that we are the only one who waits. That is never true. Even today, God is waiting for a wayward son or daughter to begin the journey home. It is not His wish that any miss the love and forgiveness He offers. A thousand years or a day are no different to Him. We may be waiting for an answer to prayer, for sickness to be healed, for a relationship to be restored, for a mate, for a child, or for a miracle that no one but God knows we need. But He is waiting for hearts of men and women to be struck by the power of His grace, and I count it a privilege to be able to wait with Him.

# A Prayer for Patience

Yahweh Rohi, *the LORD our shepherd, I lift high your name.*

*Thank You for being as patient with me as a shepherd who patiently leads his sheep. Thank You for being a God who waits with love and long-suffering kindness for men to come to the point of repentance. I am grateful for Your patience with me too, as I grow into the likeness of Your Son, Jesus Christ. The process seems so slow at times, and I can't help but think that my stumbling must try Your patience—but You never give up on me.*

*I pray today that You would teach me to imitate Your patience. That You would supply me with Your grace when I am called to wait in silence and in darkness and that You would use those waiting times to build my faith in You. I know that You are a God who is never late, but who is always right on time.*

*Lord, teach me that patience produces rest and that Your rest is something I need to strive for. The world nurtures my impatience, and it produces stress, not rest, but I know that there is rest to be found in You. Help me to resist the temptation of responding to the urgent before I attend to the important. Give me Your perspective, Father, as I seek to order my days, and let nothing come before my time with You. Amen.*

# Why Me, Lord?
## The Penny of Justice

*God will not long leave a man in trouble
whose only fear in trouble is that
he should leave the way of right.*
—Charles Spurgeon

The dictionary defines *entitlement* as proper grounds for seeking or claiming something. *Justice* is defined as the "principle or ideal of just dealing or right action," or "conformity to truth." Men and women in our day are big on entitlement, but they have lost their hunger and thirst for justice. God has always been big on justice. The Old Testament is filled with references to justice, and God continually refers to Himself as the One who executes it. The prophets hungered for it. The poor pleaded for it. The accused prayed for it. But it was the Lord who said this:

> *Let not a wise man boast of his wisdom, and let not the mighty man boast of his might, let not a rich man boast of his riches; but let him who boasts boast of this, that he understands and knows Me, that I am the LORD who exercises lovingkindness, justice, and righteousness on earth; for I delight in these things (Jer. 9:23-24, NASB).*

Clearly, justice is God's arena—and His delight—but the world that we live in is full of injustice. People who commit crimes go free on legal technicalities. People who are innocent are found guilty. Thousands of children are killed each year in the crossfire of gang warfare, and millions more die in what should be the safest place on earth—their mother's womb. Some are still persecuted even today for the color of their skin.

No one is immune from the possibility of persecution. In fact, for the Christian, persecution is a promise, not a possibility: *"Remember the word that I said to you,"* said Jesus, *'a slave is not greater than his master.' If they persecuted Me, they will also persecute you; if they kept My word, they will keep yours also. . . . They will make you outcasts from the synagogue, but an hour is coming for everyone who kills you to think that he is offering service to God. And these things they will do, because they have not known the Father, or Me"* (John 15:20; 16:2-3, NASB). *"Indeed,"* the apostle Paul wrote to his young friend Timothy, *"all who desire to live godly in Christ Jesus will be persecuted"* (2 Timothy 3:12, NASB).

In other words, expect trouble. Expect hardship. But learn to see your persecution or your trial not as a disaster but as a penny—a gift! When you are falsely accused, remember, *God is just.* When you are forgotten, remember, *God is just.* When you are hated, baited or set up, remember, *God is just.* The secret of the penny of justice is to remember that those who wait on Yaweh for justice are never disappointed.

## The Injustice of False Accusations

I know of no greater story of justice than the story of Joseph. This favorite son of Jacob experienced tremendous change throughout the course of his life. He went from a pampered existence as his father's favorite son to betrayal by his brothers in a desert pit. Then God took him from the pit to the house of Potiphar—captain of the Egyptian Pharaoh's guard. Just when life had begun to look up, Potiphar's wife falsely accused him of a crime he would rather have died than commit, but even his innocence did not keep him from being sentenced to prison. It was her word against his.

Anyone who has been falsely accused knows the anguish of injustice. Joseph was not guilty, but he suffered as if he were. But even in the jail where the king's prisoners were confined, *"the LORD was with Joseph and extended kindness to him, and gave him favor in the sight of the chief jailer. The LORD was with him; and whatever he did, the LORD made to prosper"* (Gen. 39:21, 23, NASB). The chief jailer put Joseph in charge, and didn't bother to check up on him, since he knew he was a man of character. Joseph could have screamed and raged about his circumstances, but he didn't. He could have treated everyone in the prison with him with contempt or held an attitude of superiority, but he didn't. He stayed sweet, and he became a servant:

> *In the prison's darkest hour, stay faithful, sweet and*
> *    right*
> *Keep your eyes upon the Master, no matter how*
> *    dark the night*
> *And when the tempter's snare is set your own will*
> *    to pursue*
> *Quick, to your inner chamber get, and to your Lord*
> *    be true*
> *And when the shepherd's staff is dropped, and*
> *    prison doors burst open wide*
> *You'll humbly bow your head and say, "My Lord*
> *    be glorified."*

When a fellow prisoner was released, he promised to mention Joseph's plight to Pharaoh, but two years went by, and nothing happened. No one came for him. No terms were offered for his release. Those two years must have been the toughest for Joseph. But something important happened during that time. Joseph "ceased to wait anxiously on the cupbearer and began to wait expectantly on God." In *From Bad Beginnings to Happy Endings*, Ed Young writes, "Joseph wasn't counting on family, friends or his former employer to correct the injustices of his life. He was counting on God to redeem them."[1]

God did. He used a bad dream by Pharaoh and a chance memory of the cupbearer to catapult Joseph from the dark and damp dungeon prison to the pomp and splendor of Pharaoh's palace. In a moment, his circumstances changed. The wrongs done to Joseph were made right by the God who worked justice on the earth and is still working it today.

For two years after Nancy and I married, I interrupted my education at Liberty University to work and preach in Detroit. They were tough years. We were both young and headstrong, we were poor, and we were struggling to learn to live together. I had a part-time job at a boys' home in the inner city that kept food on our table in between preaching assignments. It was during that time that I learned what it meant to be falsely accused. One of our residents in the boys' home was a big (six feet tall and 200 pounds) kid who had some learning difficulties. He wanted very much to leave the home and applied to do so, but was denied. In his anger and frustration, he attempted to get out by accusing one of the workers—me— of molesting him. No charges were ever filed, but it was one of the most devastating events of my life. I will never forget it. I certainly could not see God's hand in it, and I could not understand how He could allow this horrible thing to happen to me.

Ten years later I was preaching in Washington, D.C., and while I was there I received a call from a woman whose employer held a high-level position working with military intelligence. She was calling, she explained, to see if I might talk with her boss because he was depressed and at the end of his rope. I said that I would. Later that afternoon, the gentleman's secretary phoned. He was traveling overseas and wouldn't see me. "You tell him," I told her, "that the same thing happened to me years ago." She connected me with him, and he began to pour out a story that sounded amazingly familiar. He had been accused of raping a coworker. He was innocent, but the allegations alone stood to ruin his career, his home life, and his reputation.

"I know how this must sound," he said. "I'm sure you couldn't possibly understand how I feel." But I could. When he finished with his story, I began with mine. Before our conversation ended, he prayed to receive Jesus Christ as his Savior. He did not take his life. Today he is a trustee of the largest Baptist church in Washington, D.C., and is regarded by all who know him as a man of tremendous character.

In 1980, I could not see how God could possibly redeem the false accusations that were made against me by the young man at the boys' home. In 1990, I was actually thankful for the experience that allowed me to empathize with a man I had never met and to witness to him with rock-solid conviction about the love of God that transcends whatever tragedy life can bring. Only God could take the injustice of untrue accusations and use it for His glory, as the following poem so beautifully illustrates:

> My life is but a weaving, between my God and me;
> I do not choose the colors, He worketh steadily.
> Oftimes He weaveth sorrow, and I in foolish pride,
> Forget He sees the upper, and I the underside.
> Not till the loom is silent, and the shuttles cease to fly,
> Will God unroll the canvas, and explain the reason why.
> The dark threads are as needful in the skillful weaver's hand
> As the threads of gold and silver in the pattern He has planned.[2]

## The Injustice of Hatred

If there is a single thing more difficult to understand than blind hatred, I don't know what it is. Pictures on the nightly news of the carnage in the former Yugoslavia and Rwanda leave me reeling in sadness and confusion. I read recently in *USA Today* that American actor Harvey Keitel watched the same images that are beamed to you and me by satellite until the moment came that he thought, *I must do something*. He went to Sarajevo and saw the shrapnel-pocked buildings with their broken-out windows, empty school rooms, and emptier eyes of frightened children.[3]

"What," he asked, "is informing these people that they must have this piece of land—no matter what women and children are living on it? That they must propel steel into their bodies in order to get them off the land?" What is it that fires such intense hatred in the hearts of Serbs, Croats, and Muslims that they would murder innocent children in defense of "local gods"? Intolerance. Greed. Stubbornness. Misunderstanding. Pride. The same things that fuel hatred anywhere—in the Third World, in Eastern Europe, or in the heart of middle-America or the Southern Baptist Convention.

I learned about hatred in the same place I learned about love: the church. Nancy and I returned to Liberty University in the fall of 1980 so that I could continue my education, and once there, we became involved in a local church. While I was still a student, I became the first (and only) staff evangelist to serve at that church. I was twenty-four years old. It soon became evident that a senior member of the church staff was not pleased with my appointment and even less pleased with me. He made it his mission to make our lives unpleasant, and for a time he was quite successful.

He had me followed frequently. He started rumors that presented me in the most negative light possible. They were never about any alleged immoralities, but they were unseemly enough to plant seeds of doubt in the minds of those who did not know me well. Nancy was not immune from the unpleasantness. She was "spiritually brow-beaten" by this man and his wife, and made to feel that she never measured up to their standards as a staff wife or as a Christian. Under the guise of spiritual authority, they pressured her to toe the line they drew—and it caused her tremendous anguish. I was angry at their treatment of her and frustrated with the opposition I faced from within the church itself. Apparently this man was too powerful and visible for anyone else to confront, and by 1983 we had had enough. We left the church under a cloud of needless controversy and went back home. I eventually received my degree from Liberty, but it took a long time for the pain of that experience to fade from memory.

In 1990 I received an invitation from my alma mater to speak at a campus revival service. I had some concerns about going back, knowing that the man who had so hated Nancy and me was still serving in the church we left and held a position of leadership at the university as well. I am thankful to this day that I chose to be obedient to God's call and went. What happened there among the students that week in October was incredible.

I led student prayer meetings every day at 6:30 A.M. That's early for me—and definitely a stretch for the average college student—but the number in attendance increased steadily until Friday, when over 2,000 students participated. Hundreds of students rededicated their lives to the Lord, some accepted the call to full-time Christian service, and some realized they were simply playing the game of Christianity and accepted Christ as their Lord and Savior for the first time. Lives were changed. I know mine was. Dr. Jerry Falwell, chancellor of Liberty (and the man who was responsible for my being there as a student), said of that week: "In my eighteen years as chancellor of Liberty University, I do not remember a time when I've felt a greater emphasis and attitude toward prayer. The Lord has laid the issue of prayer on my heart. Rick Amato came here with that burden and speaker after speaker has come here with that burden. I believe the Lord is about to do something very special at Liberty University."

A short time after that, I was asked to return to Liberty to work with Dr. Falwell, and my former adversary told him, "If Rick Amato comes, I quit." He didn't have to worry; I didn't go. But he did quit—under a cloud of suspicion much more serious than the one he had tried to cast over me years before.

You see, justice is a law of God's universe, just like gravity. Justice belongs to Him, and He is much more concerned about it than you or I could ever be. My job and yours is simply to remain humble and obedient and to trust Him. Elizabeth Elliot, widow of missionary Jim Elliot, said it this way: "God is God. I dethrone Him in my heart when I demand He act in ways that satisfy my idea of justice." He has His own ideas where justice is concerned, and unlike my own, His are always right.

I cannot emphasize enough how God has crushed me time and time again through the penny of persecution only to show me, in the midst of my suffering, that its flip side is justice. His justice will roll like a mighty river. It may tarry, but it will come. Like Joseph, we need to look beyond our circumstances to the heart of a God who is always for us. We need to entrust ourselves to Him. The late Francis Schaeffer said, "When I lack proper contentment, either I have forgotten that God is God, or I have ceased to be submissive to Him. A quiet disposition and a heart giving thanks at any given moment is the real test of the extent to which we love God." The world says, "Demand your rights." God says, "Trust Me." The world says, "You're entitled." God says, "Wait on Me." The world says, "They can't treat you that way." God says, "That's how they treated Me. Trust Me. I love you. Justice is Mine."

## "God Meant It for Good"

Joseph waited on God's hand to provide justice. Imagine the scene when, years after they sold him into slavery, Joseph's brothers were brought into his presence once again. This time he was powerfully positioned as Egypt's prime minister. He controlled the nation's goods and its commerce. They were foreigners, coming to beg for bread, since their own country was still experiencing the effects of famine. He had every advantage this time. He knew them, but they did not recognize him at all. When he had heard their requests, tested their hearts, and seen his younger brother Benjamin face to face, he decided the time was right to reveal his true identity.

What happened next was proof that God had been at work in Joseph's life through every trial, every heartache, every injustice. He sent everyone but his brothers away. He called them close and began to weep so loud that the entire household heard. Then he said, "I am Joseph! Is my father still alive?" They were speechless. He drew them nearer still. "I am your brother Joseph, whom you sold into Egypt." I'm sure at this point they braced themselves for his anger. Condemnation. Accusation. Imprisonment. They knew full well what they deserved. But instead of the justice they expected, they received his mercy:

> "And now do not be grieved or angry with yourselves, because you sold me here; for God sent me before you to preserve life. For the famine has been in the land these two years, and there are still five years in which there will be neither plowing nor harvesting. And God sent me before you to preserve for you a remnant in the earth, and to keep you alive by a great deliverance. Now therefore it was not you who sent me here, but God" (Gen. 45:5-8, NASB).

His brothers might have acted years ago with evil intent, but God had meant it only for good, and Joseph knew it. He dealt kindly with them in response to God's kindness to him.

## The Justice of an Empty Tomb

The injustice Joseph suffered was certainly greater than any I have known. But there is One in history who suffered the greatest injustice of all. His name was Jesus. He was the spotless lamb, the sinless Son of God. He was sent from heaven by God for the redemption of humanity. Becoming a man was injustice enough, but He endured much more than that. Paul wrote to the Philippians that *"being found in appearance as a man, He humbled Himself by becoming obedient to the point of death, even death on a cross" (Phil. 2:8, NASB)*. He died an ugly, horrible, painful death for no just cause—except the one for which He came.

He was hunted. Taunted. Arrested. Beaten. Falsely accused. Subjected to the ridiculous charade of a mock trial. Handed over to weak and selfish men who wanted only to be rid of Him. He was hung on a Roman cross between two common criminals, underneath a sign that was meant as a punch line. He had done nothing to deserve the death penalty. He was the best this world has ever seen and will ever see. While He was dying, He spoke words of caring to His mother. He prayed for his murderers. He offered forgiveness and eternal life to one of the thieves who hung dying beside him. Then He shouted with more power than a dying man should have: *"It is finished!" (John 19:30, NASB)*.

When He did, history cracked like split ice. The veil in the temple split from top to bottom. Creation blinked, shuddered, and heaved a mighty groan. Holy God died for sinful man—on purpose. His followers didn't understand it then. The world they thought had ended had really just begun, but there was no light for them—yet. It was the darkest hour they had ever known.

Where was justice? It was being meted out in heaven, where God accepted the sacrifice of His sinless Son so that He could receive the world back to Himself. Justice was rolling down like water, and righteousness like a rolling stream. Two dark days went by, and a third dawned. The women who had loved Him went to the borrowed tomb they'd laid Him in, too hurried by the approaching Sabbath to prepare His body as they'd wished. When they arrived they found the stone that covered it rolled away, and there was no body inside. They were still heartbroken—and now confused. But then, *"two men suddenly stood near them in dazzling apparel; and as the women were terrified and bowed their faces to the ground, the men said to them, 'Why do you seek the living One among the dead? He is not here, but He has risen. Remember how He spoke to you while He was still in Galilee, saying that the Son of Man must be delivered into the hands of sinful men, and be crucified, and the third day rise again.' And they remembered His words"* (Luke 24:4-8, NASB).

Do you remember our definition of *justice*? Justice is the "principle of just dealing or right action," or "conformity to truth." There's really a much simpler definition: Justice is an empty tomb. Jesus did not deserve the death He suffered. You and I did. But He took it, and in the end, God spoke His final word in the eloquence of an empty hillside tomb. We cry out for justice so many times, and our God is just. He does deliver justice. It is His. But the better news is that His justice made it possible for you and me to receive what we really need more than we need our next breath: His mercy. How grateful I am that it is so.

## A Prayer for Justice

*I revere the name Yahweh Shalom, "The LORD our peace."*

*When it seems there is no justice, I rest in Your holy name and the peace that comes from knowing that You are my peace. Lord God, just and holy One, quiet our striving for justice in this life with the knowledge that justice will be Yours. God, You allowed Your servant Joseph to be sold as a slave, bound with fetters and laid in irons, but Your justice rolled. You allowed Your precious Son to be crucified and buried, but your justice rolled when the stone was rolled away. God, there have been times when I have longed for justice—cried for it—but I know that You meant my injustices only for good because that is what You are.*

*Almighty God, make my praise for Your mercy as deep as my cry for Your justice. I know that all that is wrong may never be made right in this place, but there is a day and there is a place where You have promised to wipe away every tear. Creation groans for that day, and my soul does too.*

*Father, teach me to treat others justly and to show them the kind of mercy that You have shown me. You have demonstrated Your love for me in the most "unjust" but incredible way: You allowed Your Son to die for me while I was still a sinner. We love because You loved us first. We love because You taught us how. Make us merciful as You are merciful. And Father, let Your justice roll. Amen.*

# Slava Bogu! (Glory to God)
## The Penny of Courage

*We think that when we suffer a defeat,*
*that all is ended. It is only a beginning, always.*
—Richard M. Nixon

It has been said that great obstacles make great men. I believe that God makes great men and women, but He uses tremendous challenges many times to do so. Challenge is often the crucible in which courage is forged— and a true man of courage is a rarity in our time. I have been privileged in my life to meet such men, but their names would not be familiar to you, or to many others. Names like Semchenko, Naprienko, Skornichov, and Kryuchkov—men who stood courageously for God in a time and place where it was dangerous to speak His name. Men who were imprisoned unjustly and persecuted regularly—and whose families suffered along with them.

Their stories are forever linked with the land from which they came, and in recent years, that land has seen radical change. Since 1989, the media has barraged the public with the breathtaking story of the demise of Communism in Eastern Europe. If you have watched a television, read a newspaper, or followed the course of world events at all, you know that the once impenetrable Berlin Wall has become a window of opportunity. That the Iron Curtain has become an open door. That millions of Russians, East Germans, Romanians, Latvians, Lithuanians, and others are experiencing freedom for the first time in decades.

I have witnessed many of these changes firsthand. A piece of the Berlin Wall sits on my desk and reminds me of the early days of East Germany's freedom. I am still amazed at the circumstances that brought me face to face with Soviet president Mikhail Sergeyevich Gorbachev just after his resignation in 1991. A framed letter written on the stationery of Leonid Brezhnev sits on the desk in my study, next to a photo of one of my heroes—Klava Goncharuk, the sixty-four-year-old woman who hid the leaders of Russia's underground church in her cellar from 1966 until 1989. These things are reminders to me that what happened to me there is real.

It is easy for those of us whose perceptions are shaped by the television reports and glossy news magazines to view these changes that have taken place in a detached way. But for those who have experienced them firsthand, they are nothing less than stunning. Once at a luncheon, I was seated near the Baroness Cox of the British House of Lords and the governor of Oradia, Romania. When the Baroness asked the governor, "Do you still believe in Communism?" his reply left little room for doubt. "I assure you, madam," he said, "you can tell Her Majesty the Queen that the only Communists left in the world are in the American institutions of higher learning."

But who is responsible for these historic changes? Do we credit *Time* magazine's former Man of the Year Mikhail Gorbachev? Was former president and outspoken opponent of Communism Ronald Reagan chiefly responsible? Or did the economic weaknesses of the Communist system itself cause its downfall? My answer today would be "none of the above." I believe instead that the God of history changed the face of His world—through the prayers of His people and the courage of a remnant of faithful believers, who persevered in the face of challenge and ultimately prevailed.

## Courage to Confront Giants

God has always called and equipped men to do His will. Usually, they are ordinary men, made extraordinary only by His touch on their lives. They are men who are not exceptionally brave—but who are made strong and courageous by the power of His Spirit. David was such a man. This shepherd boy was a true hero and the man of the hour for Israel when there was no other man willing to step to the line and defend Yahweh God in the face of a giant's threats.

The story is told in 1 Samuel 17. The setting was the valley of Elah. The armies of Israel and Philistia were camped opposite one another, and, for 39 days and 39 nights, the Philistine giant Goliath taunted the Israelite army to send someone against him. How big is a giant? This one was over nine feet tall and probably weighed in excess of 400 pounds. Where I come from, that's a big dude. His armor and sword alone weighed more than the average Israelite soldier. He proposed a one shot deal: If Israel's champion could defeat Goliath, the Philistines would concede the valley to Israel and serve them. But if Goliath was victorious, the Israelites must do likewise. Israel wasn't just threatened with a loss of honor; the nation was facing possible extinction. But in the face of her gravest challenge, no man came forward to defend her.

Their reasons for doing nothing were simple and rational. There was too much to lose. Send the wrong man, and every man would become a slave. (What they didn't know was that they were slaves already.) The giant was too big to hit and bring down. No one in Israel matched him, pound for pound or inch for inch. Negativism ruled the Israelite camp, and, as the days stretched into weeks, Goliath's daily challenge must have been a recurring source of shame and fear.

Then one morning a shepherd boy named David was sent by his father to the Israelite camp to bring food to his brothers. So he set out, carrying grilled cheese sandwiches and a sling shot. (No one ever told you about the grilled cheese sandwiches? Well, the Bible says he took an ephah of grain, ten loaves of bread, and ten cuts of cheese. In Detroit, we call that "grilled cheese.") Goliath must have been making his daily appearance just as David arrived. He listened, and his heart burned at the giant's words: *"I defy the ranks of Israel this day; give me a man that we may fight together" (V. 10).*

Then David spoke to the men standing by, as they had done day after day: *"Who is this uncircumcised Philistine, that he should taunt the armies of the living God?" (V. 26). David's brother Eliab, probably ashamed that his baby brother's outrage far exceeded his own, tried to hush him up. But his words got back to King Saul, who sent for the boy. Face to face with the man he would one day succeed as King of Israel, David spoke: "Let no man's heart fail on account of him; your servant will go and fight with this Philistine" (V. 32).* I wonder if Saul laughed? He did turn down David's offer, saying he was too young and inexperienced for giant-killing. David pointed out that since he had killed lions and bears defending his flock, he was not the least bit intimidated by an oversized, bragging Philistine.

Perhaps his final argument, though, was the one that swayed Saul in his favor. *"The LORD who delivered me from the paw of the lion and from the paw of the bear, He will deliver me from the hand of this Philistine" (V. 37).* Saul agreed, but dressed David in his own armor for good measure. (I am grateful that I am not the only man who has ever attempted to "help" God along.) David opted instead for a stripped-down approach, taking only his sling-shot and five smooth stones.

You know the story. One very small shepherd. One smooth stone. The power of God. One very dead Philistine giant. But perhaps David's greatest legacy of courage is found in the words that preceded Goliath's fall:

> *"This day the LORD will deliver you up into my hands, and I will strike you down . . . that all the earth may know that there is a God in Israel, and that all this assembly may know that the LORD does not deliver by sword or by spear; for the battle is the LORD's and He will give you into our hands"* (1 Sam. 17: 46-47, NASB).

The battle is the Lord's. God's man in this instance was an unlikely candidate to deliver a nation. But whom God prepares, God promotes. And when He does, the glory is all His. David was never confused about his part in the drama of Elah Valley. He knew it was God who fought for him, and for Israel, and won. The heroes of Russia's bulletless revolution were ordinary men who faced the giant of Communism with utter confidence in God—and He ultimately won.

## *The Courage to Venture Out*

All my life I dreamed of preaching the message of the cross in Russia. I prayed as a high school student every day for the men and women of the Soviet Union. Hundreds of times I spoke the names of political prisoners aloud to God and asked Him to set them free. I held up my hands to a map of the country and pleaded, "Russia, you will let those people go. You will open the doors to God and the gospel." When the editor of my high school yearbook asked for my goal after graduation, I said "I'm going to Russia to preach the gospel." (I'm sure my classmates thought my earlier drug use had taken its toll.)

My first opportunity to visit the country I'd prayed so fervently for came in 1986. A brush with serious illness sobered me up, and I realized that life is short. I cashed in what frequent-flyer miles I had and decided it was time to go. I went to Lynchburg Virginia to confer with Jerry

Falwell Jr., my long-time friend and counselor who was
at that time chairman of my board of directors. "Jerry," I
said, "I'm going to Russia."

"Going where, Rick?"

"I'm going to Russia to preach the cross."

"You know somebody in Russia?" he asked.

"No," I said, "I don't know anybody in Russia."

He could see that this was going to take some explaining. "Rick," he said, "if you were to get put in jail in the
States, chances are I could get you out." (Jerry's a lawyer,
and a good one.) "But if you're put in jail in Russia, even
the President of the United States couldn't get you out.
These people have nuclear weapons. They don't like
Christians. And if they find out why you're there, they
will put you in jail. So my advice to you is, don't go to
Russia."

"I'm going, Jerry," I said.

"We can't sanction it as a board Rick. But I'll tell you
what—there's a man by the name of Vernon Brewer. He's
been smuggling Bibles into Russia for years. Maybe Vernon would let you go along with him."

Vernon Brewer was taking the Word of God into
Russia before just about anyone. He took great risks to
bring Bibles to the Soviet people, exhibiting the courage
to venture out of his own personal "safety zone" to do so
time and again. Jerry told him about me, and Vernon
invited me along on his next trip. He told me he planned
to take 300 Bibles on this particular trip.

"Why don't we take 10,000?" I asked.

"Ten thousand? How are we going to get 10,000
Bibles into Russia?"

"Well," I reasoned, "everybody's going to take suitcases, right? Why don't we take two suitcases each, and
fill one with clothes and the other one with Bibles?"

"What if we get caught?" Vernon asked.

"Have you ever gotten caught?" I asked him.

"No. Well, a couple of times."

"What did they do?" I asked.

"They threatened us. And in Romania they held me at submachine-gun-point at the border. I thought they were going to kill me."

"But they didn't," I said, stating the obvious.

"No, of course not."

"Then let's do it," I said.

Vernon, being the wiser of the two of us, was certainly the braver. I was just naive. But we wrote letters to each of the thirty-five people who were coming with us, telling them to bring two suitcases and to put clothes in only one of them. I talked to our RAM treasurer and told him I needed $35,000 to buy 10,000 Russian New Testaments and 3,000 Romanian Bibles. He said we didn't have the money to buy 35 Bibles, in Russian, Romanian, or any other language.

Just a short time earlier, I had agreed to appear on the PTL program. Jim Bakker had been indicted, but the show was still on, and different evangelists were filling in. I gave my testimony, then I told the television audience our plans to go to Russia and Romania in a few weeks. The phone lines lit up and callers donated money for our trip, although I never requested it. One of my close friends, Tim Duggins, was working closely at that time with Dr. Herbert Fitzpatrick, a pastor from Maryland who was to become one of my dearest mentors. These men voluntarily collected over $50,000 in donations. The rocket was launched.

Our party arrived in Moscow with suitcases crammed full of Bibles. We must have had the heaviest luggage on record. I was pushed to the front of the line to be cleared by the border guards, and all I could think of was my suitcase full of Bibles. My knees were shaking so hard that my teeth chattered as I smiled. Everything I saw was red. Red doors. Red ropes. Red stars on the hats of the Russian security officers. The first guard immediately opened my Bible suitcase. I thought, *This is it. It's all over.* But as soon as I saw his face, I knew I was wrong.

The look that registered was one not of rage—but one of thirst!

I wondered what his response would be, but before I could speak, a voice inside me said, "What does it matter? Give him one." I reached into the suitcase and handed him one of the Bibles. He grabbed it and stashed it quickly under a table, out of sight. Then he looked at this long line of terrified, grinning Americans, each with two suitcases, and barked out to the other officers, "Amerikanskis—let them through." They never checked another suitcase. Thirty-five of us walked into the Soviet Union with 10,000 copies of the Word of God. We were tourists by day. And we smuggled Bibles every night.

One of the most fascinating passages of Scripture I know is Hebrews 11. Men and women of faith are chronicled there for eternity, and the actions that merited God's pleasure are spelled out clearly. Hebrews 11:8 says that *"By faith Abraham, when he was called, obeyed by going out to a place which he was to receive for an inheritance; and he went out, not knowing where he was going"* (NASB). Today it's a shameful thing for a man not to know where he is going, but Abraham's lack of assurance required faith—a quality that pleases Almighty God, then and now. Abraham had the courage to venture out. Vernon Brewer had it too. Many others do as well—heroes whose names are unknown to you and me and will be until God reveals them in praise as He did the saints in Hebrews 11.

### *"Is This Your Suitcase?"*

I had gotten the name of an unregistered Russian church from a man who immigrated to the United States and was sponsored by my home church. It is important to note that there were three "churches" in Russia at that time. The registered church obeyed the government and did most of what the KGB demanded. Some of their pastors were, in fact, KGB agents. The autonomous church, a group of Christians who were just emerging,

SLAVA BOGU! (GLORY TO GOD)    111

was headed by Alexander Semchenko, a Soviet business-
man. This man ultimately became my partner and was
the driving force behind most of what we did in Russia.
He founded a new denomination of Protestants that
Americans really liked. They were independent, unaffili-
ated with any official church or religion. The third group
was the unregistered church. This was the Christian underground. They met in secret. They evangelized. Their
leader, Genady Kruchkov, was one of the most hunted
men in Russia. The KGB to this day would like to know
how he eluded them for so many years.

I went to Vernon and told him I wanted to take a
suitcase full of Bibles to this unregistered church. I asked
him to go with me. "You know those people are illegal,"
he said. "They're considered criminals, and you will be
too if you're caught." But he gave me permission to go.
He stayed with our group, thinking that if we were both
arrested there would be no one to shepherd them back to
the States. Bob Lauro, a producer, and Gene Howes, two
cowboy television men from Liberty Broadcasting Net-
work, were already grabbing their gear to go along.

The trip to a nondescript high-rise should have taken
no more than 25 minutes, but we wound through the
streets of Moscow for two hours, trying to elude the KGB
agents who were certainly following us. I'll never forget
the sight of these persecuted believers. They sat on two-
by-fours stretched between chairs. When I opened the
suitcase full of Bibles, grown men wept out loud. Tears
flowed like water that night. I met the pastors and remembered the nights I had prayed in my room in Detroit
for them and for men like them.

By the end of the week, we had smuggled more Bibles
to more unregistered groups, but somehow, on the last
night of my first trip, an empty suitcase was lost.

What I'm going to tell you now will sound like something out of a movie. I assure you, it is not. A man named
John Loyd witnessed the entire episode from behind the
corner. As I was packing to return home, I noticed three

spare Bibles. Thinking they were meant as souvenirs, I packed them as well. Then I heard a knock at the door. I opened it to the biggest, tallest, most intimidating character I had ever seen. His two "friends" standing behind him were bigger still. He spoke perfect English. "I hope you have enjoyed your stay in the Soviet Union," he said. "I am with the security police." My knees began to shake and my heart pounded. He was KGB. I knew it.

"I understand you have lost a suitcase," he continued. "May I ask you what was in that suitcase?"

"Nothing," I squeaked, without much conviction.

He wasn't buying it. "Do you always carry an empty suitcase around Moscow? What was in the suitcase?"

I started to do what most preachers confronted with a call to a Siberian prison ministry would do—lie—but I couldn't. "Would you excuse me a moment?" I asked. "I need to go to the bathroom." Then I closed the door. "Oh Jesus," I cried, "it's the KGB! What am I going to do?" Then I heard a gentle whisper in my soul say, "Those three Bibles are not souvenirs." I took them out of my suitcase, took a deep breath, and opened the door. Still there. I figured as much.

Looking into the agent's face, I began to speak. "Mister," I said, "I'm not going to lie to you. My name's Rick Amato, and I'm a preacher of the cross. I came to tell the people of your country that there is a God, He is real, He loves you, and that Jesus died on the cross to prove it. And that when He rose again, He proved He was real. I want you to know that He made a way for you to know Him and to find forgiveness for your sin and deliverance for your life." I held one of the Bibles out to him. "This is called the Bible. It tells the whole story, which hopefully you'll need because, hopefully, I plan to be leaving tomorrow. I'd like to tell you more, but everything you need for life is in this book." I'm sure I was speaking faster than the speed of light. I didn't wait for a response. "Here's one for each of your friends too," I said as I pressed the Bibles into his enormous hands.

He took the Bibles and pulled them close to his chest. Then tears welled up in his eyes. "Oh, thank you, sir," he cried. "In my country this is the most precious gift a man could ever receive." Then he pulled out a card and wrote something on the back of it. As he handed it to me, he said, "Here, take this. It is my name and the telephone number where I live. If you have any problem in Russia, you call me." I assured him that I would.

There is a force alive today that is more powerful than nations or ideologies or man-made laws. It is man's instinctive hunger to know God. I have seen it all over the world, and I can assure you that its expression goes beyond language and culture. Many never see it, though, because they lack the courage to venture out in faith. The next time you face a challenge that seems impossible, venture out. Then watch expectantly to see what God will do.

## *Along for the Ride*

Things began to snowball after that for RAM and Russia. Looking back on the events that followed my first trip to the Soviet Union, I see that God was in control and that I was simply along for the ride. We made four trips to Eastern Europe in eighteen months. A meeting was organized in Moscow's Zvozney Hall, and I was invited to speak on the existence of God. I appeared on "120 Minutes"—the Russian equivalent of "Good Morning America"—and other news talk shows, and was able to give my testimony to nearly 300 million potential television viewers several different times.

Then organizers proposed renting Olympic Stadium, a sports venue for 50,000, to hold a crusade. I didn't think we could fill it. But I noticed on my first trip to Russia that there wasn't much food available to the masses. On my second trip, I had taken along some Spam—three or four cans—and people loved it! (I know it's hard to imagine, but they got as excited about Spam as I do about a big lobster!) So I began telling my friends back home, "Just give me a few cans of Spam, and let me go." What happened was crazy. I started getting Spam. Lots of it. From everywhere. People from Maine to California and from Florida to Washington heard what we were doing and sent us Spam. I told people, "Send Spam to RAM for the glory of the Lamb!" I know it sounds crazy, but it worked! We put thousands of cans of the stuff on a boat and shipped it over to Russia. When the time came for the crusade, Olympic Stadium was almost half full. We saw nearly 15,000 people saved. Then I got a message from Alexander Semchenko, the previously mentioned head of the autonomous church and supporter of Boris Yeltsin. They wanted to hold a crusade in the Kremlin!

Changes had taken place in Russia. Gorbachev had resigned. Boris Yeltsin was the new president. A wind of religious awakening had stirred the hearts of many, and there was an amazing openness to the things of God. A "sanctifying concert" had been planned for the Kremlin, and they wanted a preacher—but not a famous one or a political one. So they chose the most unlikely one imaginable: me. When they did, they assured that God and God alone would receive the glory for what took place. I was an unknown; I was no one of significance or power.

People from all over America responded, sending food and supplies to the masses. Across the denominational spectrum, the Christians of America supported the presenting of the cross in the Kremlin by sending help. Pat Robertson, a great American, and CBN's Operation Blessing were especially generous, as were Southern Baptists across America.

The hopes of these Christians were not disappointed.

For four nights the people came. The face of Lenin came down from the blue curtain where it had hung for fifty years in the Kremlin, and the cross of Christ replaced it. High government officials were in attendance. The wife of President Boris Yeltsin came, along with fifty members of his family and staff. Vice President Alexander Rutskoi and his wife were there. (Rutskoi was later arrested as one of the leaders of the 1993 parliamentary rebellion and has since been granted amnesty.) Over 24,000 people participated in powerful praise and worship. Almost as many said yes to Jesus Christ as their Lord and Savior.

Then, to my amazement, after some inquiry on my part, I learned that arrangements had been made for me to meet with former president Mikhail Gorbachev. I spent twenty-five minutes in the presence of this man, whom the *Dallas Times Herald* called "the most formidable political figure since Winston Churchill." If pictures and recordings did not exist of our exchange, I might not believe myself that it took place. He asked what brought me to Russia, and I explained that I came on behalf of the Christians in America, to bring "bricks" for a foundation of liberty. He jokingly said, "Not bricks to hit people over the head with, I hope! There are some people in this country who need that, you know." Then he spoke these words as we sat down: "You are working in a field which is particularly important. You are working to strengthen the commitment to human values . . . what you are doing and what you are trying to convey to the people is very important . . . and I would like to salute you."

He talked of the absolute necessity of reform in his country and their repeated attempts to do so. I interrupted, telling him that you don't reform societies, you reform individuals, and that real reformation would come one individual at a time through the message of the death, burial and resurrection of Jesus Christ. "God has been with Russia," I said. "God will be with Russia. He is with Russia now." After signing a Bible for me and personally autographing a picture for each of my children, Mr. Gorbachev remarked, "Our grandchildren read the Bible everyday."

*"Slava bogu!"* I responded. "Glory to God."

*"Slava bogu,"* Mikhail Gorbachev said. And he smiled back at me.

## Courage to Endure

It takes a certain courage to confront giants like David did and to venture out into the unknown like Abraham did. But it takes an equal amount of courage to endure the daily hardships of life faithfully and not "fold" in the face of adversity. This is a lesson in courage that I learned from my mother.

Mom and Dad divorced when I was a teenager. I was the fifth of seven children born to Betty Jo Amato, and she became a single parent when five of us were still living at home. Some kids *think* their mom is a drill sergeant—but ours really was! Mom served as a U.S. Marine in Korea, and she was a fighter by nature. Today she battles cancer with as much courage as she once fought to keep our family together. She did whatever it took. Her first job was flipping burgers for ninety cents an hour. (Her raise to one dollar an hour was a big deal!) Mom taught me that the honor of a job was in doing the work, not in being noticed; however, someone must have noticed her because she eventually became a district manager, supervising many locations. Eventually she owned her own Burger King franchise—and until she became ill, she managed its $1.2-million-a-year operation.

Mom gave to her children before she took care of herself. I remember the night she went to bed crying because her hands were chapped and bleeding from walking to work in the cold. But every one of her kids had a pair of gloves. At twenty-eight, she was diagnosed with ovarian cancer and doctors told her she had only a short time to live. Today at sixty, she faces another fight against life-threatening cancer, but no one is talking about time. Mom will live until God calls her home.

Never once has she questioned any of my decisions or tried to discourage me from following God's call on my life. Some said our trips to Russia and Cuba were dangerous and ill-advised, but she knew better than to focus on the negatives. She would have given up long ago if that was her way. Instead, her endurance against tremendous odds has changed my perspective on life's challenges.

Today, with five children and a wife, I am only beginning to understand what it must have taken for my mother to just keep going in those trying times. She did alone what Nancy and I do together. And she did it one day at a time. She got up each morning, worked diligently at her job, provided for her children, and then did it again the next day— and the day after that. No one applauded. There were no ruffles and flourishes. But in her courage, God was glorified.

I don't know what challenges you may be facing today—but I know this. You can take courage in the person of Jesus Christ, who, for the joy set before Him, courageously endured the cross, so that you and I could know God. We can take courage in the fact that our God is truly the God of history—and if He can change the course of nations, He can change the course of lives. And He does. *Slava bogu!* Glory to God!

# A Prayer for Courage

*God, I lift up and exalt the name of Yahweh Adoni, The LORD our master. You are the Sovereign Lord!*

*Please give us courage to face the challenges of life. Help us to embrace them, not to run from them, knowing that You are our sovereign help, and that no plan of Yours can be thwarted. When the way seems impossible and our hearts shrink, fill us with the bold assurance that You fight for us, like You fought through a shepherd boy for Israel. When opposition comes from every side, keep our eyes on You. When the world says a giant is too big to hit, whisper to us that he is simply too big to miss!*

*Precious Father, when we hear Your voice, help us to venture out—beyond what we can see. It is enough that You call. That You go before us is all we need to know. Remind us that the safest place that we can be is in the center of Your will. And when we think that we can't go on another day, God, give us the courage to endure. Whatever life holds, You are there. You have promised that nothing—death, life, angels, principalities, things present, things to come, height, depth, any created thing—can separate us from Your love. That fact should give us courage when all other hope fails.*

*"Through life, death, through sorrow and through sinning, Christ shall suffice me, for He hath sufficed; Christ is the end, for Christ was the beginning, Christ the beginning, for the end is Christ." In this, we take courage. Amen.*

# The Greatest of These

## The Penny of Love

*Little children, let us not love with word*
*or with tongue, but in deed and truth.*
1 John 3:18

Rodney King probably never intended to be famous. But when an onlooker videotaped his apprehension and arrest by Los Angeles police officers in 1991, millions of Americans became familiar with his face, his case, and the havoc its outcome rained on the city of Los Angeles. When jurors initially decided in favor of the officers who arrested him, the city saw its first race riots since Watts burned in the 1960s. Images of flaming storefronts, roadblocks, looting, shootings, and beatings were played and replayed by the national media, just as the tape from King's arrest had been months before. King himself went before cameras while the fires were still burning and tearfully implored the citizens of L.A. (and the nation), "Can't we all just, you know, get along with each other?"

It was a deceptively profound question. A loaded question. It was asked only hypothetically, perhaps, but it hit at the very heart of what's wrong with our society. It's tough, Rodney. We can't seem to love one another—at least not for very long. Evidently, our problem is not a new one. When the aging apostle John wrote his last words to the early church, love was his recurring theme. *"If we love one another, God abides in us, and his love has been perfected in us" (1 John 4:12, NASB); "He who loves his brother abides in light . . .(1 John 2:10, NASB); "Anyone who does not practice righteousness is not of God, nor is he who does not love his brother" (1 John 3:10, NASB); "And this is His Commandment, that we believe in the name of His Son Jesus Christ, and Love one another, as He gave us commandment" (1 John 3:23, NASB); "Beloved let us love one another, for love is of God; and everyone who loves is born of God and knows God" (1 John 4:7, NASB).*

Tradition has it that when St. John was very old (in his nineties), the young ministers would carry him on a mat to the services at the church at Ephesus. As they carried him, and all through their meetings, all he would say was, "Love one another! Love one another! Love one another!" The apostle's one-note theme caused many to think that he had become senile and could not help repeating himself. "What else, John?" they supposedly asked him, and his reply carried with it the authority of the last living eyewitness to the incarnate Love of God: "This is enough," he said. "There is nothing else."

Jesus too spoke chiefly of love in his last recorded conversation with His disciples, only hours before His crucifixion. *"If anyone loves Me,"* He said, *"he will keep My word; and My Father will love him, and We will come to him, and make Our abode with him. He who does not love Me does not keep My words; and the word which you hear is not Mine, but the Father's who sent Me" (John 14:23-24, NASB).* He could have dictated a church building manual, or reviewed evangelistic approaches, or had them memorize His choicest sayings in their last moments together as teacher and disciples. But the Son of God did none of these. Instead, He emphasized how critical it would be in the days, weeks, and years ahead for them to love each other. By their love, He explained, the world would know that they were His disciples. By keeping His commandments, they could demonstrate their love for God and abide in His love. Love was the key.

We live in a day and age when "believers" in Jesus are known by their adherence to a particular set of cultural preferences. We reason that if someone holds to a creed intellectually, then he or she is a "Christian." Most of what we call Christian conversion today is merely cognitive assent to a particular creed followed by conformity to a set of cultural preferences that is predetermined by the particular sect of Christianity the individual has come into contact with.

Jesus said that the mark of a Christian would be love, period. "'By this all men will know that you are My disciples, if you have love for one another'" (John 13:35, NASB). How sad that we have, in the name of the One who said this, maimed, mauled, and mainly ignored one another over non-essential issues. We are supposed to be known by our love for each other!

Many of us would say that we are more familiar with rejection than we are with real genuine love. Criminal defenses today are built around the contention that the accused was rejected or unloved by a parent or guardian early in life and so not responsible for whatever hatred he or she has spewed out at society. But the truth is, there's not a person alive who has not, at one time or another, felt unloved. We are imperfect, flawed human beings surrounded by other imperfect, flawed beings. But that is no excuse for hatred.

Paul's belief that "all have sinned and fall short of the glory of God," (Rom. 3:23, NASB) describes every living human being on earth. When we pray, "Forgive us our trespasses as we forgive those who have trespassed against us," we should be reminded that we're in the same boat with all the other sinners under the sun. Yet instead of recognizing our universal frailties and weaknesses and humbly loving people, we rage against others when they hurt us. We turn our backs on them when they disappoint us. We freeze them out when they try to reach

us and we hate them simply because they remind us of
ourselves. Still, the Bible exhorts us to love. How do we
do it?

## Admit Our Ignorance

First, we must admit that we don't really know what
love is. Our culture and popular media have distorted
our perception of love. A "love psychic" on an afternoon
talk show predicts whether a couple's romance will succeed or fail. People look for love through the "personals"
in newspapers throughout the country. Television shows
like "Melrose Place" or "Beverly Hills 90210" broadcast
their own version of love in the '90s to teenagers and
young adults each week. But love is not romance. Please
don't misunderstand—I'm all for romance. Romance is
great. But after fifteen years of marriage and raising five
kids with my wife, I can tell you that love is a whole lot
more than romance.

Love is not sex, either. Pastor/writer Calvin Miller
says it this way: "Love is substance, lust illusion. Only in
the surge of passion do they mingle in confusion."

I am frequently amazed at the way words and
phrases take on new meanings. If I hear someone say,
"We made love," I understand them to mean they had
sex. If someone else were to say about a woman, "I knew
her," I would think they had only met previously. On the
other hand, the biblical expression "Adam knew Eve"
meant that the two of them were sexually intimate. That
"knowing" was a deep and profound joining of two
souls, not a thirty-second introduction culminating in a
handshake. Sex is a deeply profound, completely bind-
ing, physical, emotional, and spiritual experience. But it
is not always love, or only love.

To add to the confusion, bumper stickers today proclaim that the car's occupant "loves" everything from
New York to cocker spaniels. But love is not a fondness
for something, either. At its heart, love is an action, inde-

pendent of any expected response. The Bible says, *"This is love: not that we loved God, but that he loved us and sent his Son as an atoning sacrifice for our sins"* (1 John 4:10, NIV). Love is a commitment to meet the true needs of another person by the power of the Holy Spirit. God's version of it worked this way: when you were a sinner, on your way to hell, when you were lost and gave no thought to God, He acted on your behalf. He sent His only Son to die for you *because you needed Him to*.

Whether or not you accept the gift of salvation that came through His Son's sacrifice, it was given to you. Your response does not change His love. Paul wrote, *"But God demonstrates His own love toward us, in that while we were yet sinners, Christ died for us"* (Rom. 5:8, NASB).

God sent His Son to die for me before I recognized my need for a Savior. His Son died for me even though I was hostile toward Him. He met me and saved me in a little church in Detroit, knowing that the only reason I had come was to make fun of Him. My response did not affect the quality of His love. It still doesn't. He loved you too, before you were born. He knew full well that you might reject Him one day. He knew of the possibility that you might deal treacherously with Him. But God committed Himself in love to meet your needs through the life, death, and resurrection of His Son. That is love.

## Learn What Not to Love

Sometimes it's easier to know what to do when we're told what not to do. If I see a sign on the highway (facing me) that says, "Wrong way," I know I'm not where I should be (or at least that I'm not heading in the direction that I should). John helped show the early church the way to love by telling them what *not* to love. *"Do not love the world, nor the things in the world,"* he wrote. *"If anyone loves the world, the love of the Father is not in him"* (1 John 2:15, NASB).

If I am in love with the world, I'm not in love with Jesus. Why? Because the things of the world—the lust of the flesh, the lust of the eyes and the boastful pride of life—are worldly things, not godly things. There is no point in loving the things of the world, too, because *they are passing away*. If I love the things of the world, I am loving things that will never last. A picture I saw recently in the paper illustrated this principle beautifully. George Swanson, a beer distributor from Hempfield Township, Pennsylvania, died at the age of seventy-one. He loved something that was passing away: his 1984 silver Corvette. He loved it so much, in fact, that he requested to be buried in it. The Associated Press wirephoto showed a hoist lowering the car—topped by a spray of red roses and containing Swanson's cremated remains—into a large burial plot. He'll always be assured of a parking space, I guess, but there's no future for a buried car—even an expensive one. It is passing away.

There is nothing in this world that is permanent. It has been said that the only things that last are the souls of men and the Word of God. Everything else will end with time. So to give our hearts to anything less is to ensure that we will lose our investment of love. No worldly cause, however noble, is worthy of my love. Only God, His book, and His people are worth investing a lifetime in loving.

## Go to the Source

I've heard some respected preachers and teachers say that for us to learn to love, we need a fresh baptism of the Holy Spirit, enabling us to speak in tongues. Others say we need signs and wonders and the working of great miracles. Still others say that love can be taught through more education, knowledge, and information. Every day I become more and more convinced that the prescription for our nation, the medicine for our troubled world, the healing balm that the church so desperately needs, is a fresh baptism of the love of God!

My generation of Americans has been led to believe that if we profess all the right doctrines, ascribe to all the right ideals, and hold to all the right theology, we *must* know God. It's just not so. It is possible to know a great deal about God and not know Him. You or I can have more degrees than a thermometer and be able to quote from more theologians than a senior pastor and bust hell's gates wide open! There will be only one "special interest" group in heaven. It will be those whose special interest was in being washed by the blood of the Lamb, Jesus Christ, and being filled with the love of God. Only those who are born of Him are able to love—and those who cannot are not His. As the apostle John reasoned: *"We love, because He first loved us"* (1 John 4:19, NASB).

Only when we know the love of God in Jesus Christ are we truly able to love others as He commands. Our love for one another becomes proof that God dwells in us and that His love is being perfected in us. We are no longer trying to "make" love or conjure it up where none exists. We are simply allowing His love to proceed from our hearts where He resides as King. You and I know this kind of love when we see it, and the world does too. It is so extraordinary, so different from the run-of-the-mill, pedestrian stuff we call love that it startles, amazes, and sometimes even offends.

Mary of Bethany exhibited this no-holds-barred kind of love when she poured costly perfume out on the feet of Jesus just before His last Passover. She lavished no less than a pound of the fragrant substance on him and wiped His feet with her hair, filling the entire house with the sweet smell of adoration. But some were offended. Most felt that her actions were embarrassing and wasteful. When Judas spoke out in protest, Jesus defended her: *"Let her alone, she has kept this for the day of My burial"* (John 12:7, NASB). Oswald Chambers wrote of the incident in *My Utmost for His Highest,* saying, "If . . . love does not carry a man beyond himself, it is not love. If love is always discreet, always wise, always sensible and calculating, never carried beyond itself, it is not love at all. It may be affection, it may be warmth of feeling, but it has not the true nature of love in it."[1] The love Mary exhibited was the love of Christ, who had entered her very heart with His love and taken up residence there.

That is the kind of love we are called to give to one another. When you and I love our neighbors, our friends, our wives, our children, our brothers, and our sisters with the love of Christ, we are obeying God's commandment to us and thus proving our love for Him. I may never get to meet Rodney King. But I would like to answer his question, "Can't we all get along?" The following ten points are suggestions as to how we can "flesh out" the love of Christ in our own lives. They are not revolutionary in their content—but when the world sees them lived out, they are revolutionary in practice. Just try them and see.

## How to Get Along: Ten Steps toward Love

Step #1 **Focus more on people's good points than on their bad ones.** When I was twenty-seven, God healed me of a life-threatening disease—a miracle for which I will always praise Him. But even more than I needed His healing from Crohn's disease, I need His healing from my bitterness, envy, jealousy, and unforgiveness. I want to look at others through the same "love-washed eyes" that God looks through when He sees me. When God spoke of David, He never said, "Behold, an adulterer and murderer!" That was David at his worst. Instead, He said, "Behold, a man after My own heart." That was David at his best. He sees not what we sometimes are, but what we can become through His grace. We ought also to look at each other in the same way.

Step #2 **Realize that love and unity are in our own best interest.** Christians are invincible when they are inseparable. The greatest protection for any church is not a great pastor, or a fine building, or huge offerings. Churches survive when their congregations truly love one another. As I've travelled around the world, one thing is certain: were the church of Jesus Christ ever to unite, it would be indomitable. Before we allow our differences to divide us, we need to take them to the cross and leave them there. The same principle of unity holds true in families, in marriages, and in friendships. It was unity that Jesus prayed for for His followers in His high priestly prayer of John 17: *"That they may all be one; even as Thou, Father, art in Me, and I in Thee, that they also may be in Us; that the world may believe that Thou didst send Me. And the glory which Thou hast given Me I have given to them; that they may be one, just as We are one"* (vv. 21-22, NASB).

Ideal Christian love and unity are realized in a Christian marriage. Though Nancy and I are not always happy with one another, we are always one. We do not always agree, but we are always one. We know that the commitment that we made to live with one another for life is in our best interest, and we are determined to protect it above all else.

Step #3 **Concentrate upon God's commands to love one another.** I would be untruthful if I said I have never had a problem with another believer, with my wife, or with a member of my family. (I say if you're married and you claim you never argue, one of you is unnecessary—or both of you are lying!) Wherever there are two minds and two wills, you can be certain that there will at times be two opinions. But we have the most powerful force in the universe at our disposal during those times, and that force is the will of God. Each time Satan goads us to condemn or hate or despise someone, we need to hear the will of God: *"This is My commandment, that you love one another"* (John 15:12, NASB). His command is bigger than our differences. It alone should be our "referee" when we are not in agreement.

Step #4 **Emphasize your agreement over your disagreement.** Being a Baptist preacher, I know plenty of Baptists. I know Free Will Baptists, Southern Baptists, Independent Baptists, Regular Baptists, General Baptists, and a lot more. Most of these fine people agree upon the major issues of theology and church life—but you'd never know it by talking with some of them! Paul's philosophy regarding the issues of the faith is worthwhile to consider: in the essentials—doctrine, the authority of the Word, etc.—he urged unity. In the nonessentials—"meat eating," traditions, etc.—he urged liberty. But in all things, Paul said, we must love:

> *If I speak with the tongues of men and of angels,* he wrote, *but do not have love, I have become a noisy gong or a clanging cymbal. And if I have the gift of prophecy, and know all mysteries and all knowledge; and if I have all faith, so as to remove mountains, but do not have love, I am nothing. And if I give all my possessions to feed the poor, and if I deliver my body to be burned, but do not have love, it profits me nothing (1 Cor. 13:1-3, NASB).*

Be more willing to celebrate your agreement than to argue your disagreement.

Step #5 **Keep peace with God.** Proverbs 16:7 says, *"When a man's ways are pleasing to the LORD, He makes even his enemies to be at peace with him"* (NASB). When we are at peace with God, we will be at peace with men—but when we give up our peace with God, we forfeit our peace with men as well. I've discovered that if I am diligent in maintaining my vertical relationship with Him, He will enable me to maintain my horizontal relationships with others. Jesus established my peace with God as Paul noted in Romans 5:1, but I must maintain it by confessing my sins and asking for His forgiveness, reading His Word, and communicating with Him in prayer. As I become more deeply aware of and grateful for God's mercy in dealing with me, I am better able to love others in a similar way.

Step #6 **Realize how related and interconnected we are to one another.** Christians exhibit an amazing tendency at times to shoot their wounded. Given the choice between restoration and extermination, we often go for the extreme! Yet God's Word says that it is good and pleasant for us to dwell together in unity. When a fellow Christian is hurt or has fallen, we are to restore them. We are to offer a place for healing. Why? Because we're fellow sufferers. We each face the same enemies—the world, the flesh, and the devil himself. And we follow the same captain, the Lord Jesus Christ. Soldiers in foxholes don't shoot each other, they band together against the enemy. So should we.

In honor of the fiftieth anniversary of D-Day, three veteran paratroopers (each now in his seventies) traveled to Europe and parachuted together over the Normandy beachhead they had once taken in the Allied invasion. Five decades had gone by, but the events of that day so bonded these three men that they remained "joined" for life. A single day of fierce battle and shed blood forged their lifelong union. We are joined too, related and interconnected to every other believer by the shed blood of the Lord Jesus Christ, who fought and bled and died for us on Calvary. We cannot afford to lose a single one He suffered for in our great cause.

Step #7 **Be aware of the misery of discord.** When I travel, I call my wife several times a day. People sometimes comment on this fact, and ask about my phone bill in a "polite" kind of way. (No one ever offers to pay it, but they are curious about it.) When someone says, "Isn't that expensive?" I usually respond, "Yes, it is—but it's cheaper than alimony!" Nancy and I know from our experience with family and friends that marital discord causes great misery. We know that it carries a high price tag. That's a great incentive at times to avoid it!

I've seen discord in churches too, and it is equally miserable for all involved. I've never seen a church split that looked like fun. When marriages fail, when families break apart, when churches split, men and women are left with broken hearts. Not just some of the time, but *all* of the time. Often the cause of Christ is damaged in the process. I believe that if we considered beforehand the cost of discord, we would fight far fewer battles of "principle" and stage far fewer "turf wars." The price is simply too high.

Step #8 **Realize that it's good to be the first to seek peace.** Jesus said, *"Blessed are the peacemakers, for they shall be called sons of God" (Matt. 5:9, NASB)*. Maybe as you've read this chapter, someone for whom you're harboring hatred has come to mind. Could you go to them and seek to make peace? Perhaps you have resentment toward someone who hurt you physically or emotionally when you were a child or toward a mate who was unfaithful or a friend who was disloyal. Or maybe you are jealous or envious toward someone who has no idea that you secretly wish they would fail. Can you find it in yourself to reach out right now to that person?

Love is a fruit of the Holy Spirit working in our lives. If there is no love giving evidence that we are born from above, we are right to question our standing in Him. Being the first to seek peace is not a sign of weakness, it is a badge of love. Don't wait. Do it now. Whatever the problem is, in the name of Jesus Christ, love one another. In the power of the Holy Spirit, reach out and do whatever it takes to make peace—even if it means being the first to say, "I was wrong."

Step #9 **Make the Word of God your touchstone.** A touchstone is a place where we stand and begin. The Bible is my touchstone. It is a marvelous piece of work, 1500 years in the making, with forty-five different authors and sixty-six different books. It contains the truth about how life works and offers utterly reliable guidance for living. The Bible reveals who God is and how He works in the world. I stand firmly on it and believe every word of it. It is the point from which I begin any serious search for truth. By balancing everything against what His Word says, we are able to love others as Christ loved us, holding *His* standard highest, not our own.

Step #10 **Spend some time examining yourself.** It will be impossible to love others as God commands if you have not received Jesus Christ as your personal Savior and allowed Him to be the Lord of your life. If you find it difficult to love, ask yourself, "Have I received Jesus? Have I chosen to walk with Him on the narrow road?" If you have not, are you willing to do so? If you are sure that you have His forgiveness and that He lives in your heart, thank Him for His presence that makes it possible to love. Don't allow anything to stem the flow of His love through you. Pray the words David spoke thousands of years ago: *"Search me, O God, and know my heart; Try me and know my anxious thoughts; And see if there be any hurtful way in me, and lead me in the everlasting way"* (Ps. 139:23-24, *NASB*).

Praying that prayer is asking God to shine light into the shadowy corners of the inner man. It is inviting Him to reveal to us areas of unconfessed sin, stunted spiritual growth, or unloving attitudes toward others. It is saying that you are willing to forgive, if that is what God calls you to do.

## *Love Never Fails*

When we look around us at all the hatred, pain, and injustice in the world, it's easy to believe that love will never prevail. But there are times when love triumphs— and in the most unlikely circumstances. Like the 1994 National Religious Broadcasters' prayer breakfast, where a tiny nun silenced an entire hall of dignitaries with the raw power of her words of love. Barely visible over the podium, she stood and read from Matthew 25 of the coming judgment, when Christ will separate those who knew and loved Him from those who did not, as a shepherd separates sheep from goats.

The president and vice president and evangelical leaders had danced carefully around each other at this highly visible event, choosing their words carefully to avoid any unpleasantness. But Mother Teresa, with the Bible as her touchstone, chose her words for their truth, not for their political correctness: "The greatest destroyer of peace today is abortion," she said. "[For] if we accept that a mother can kill even her own child, how can we tell people not to kill each other?" And then to anyone who might be considering abortion, Mother Teresa added this plea: "Please don't kill the child. I want the child. Please give me the child." Then she told of young, pregnant women she had cared for herself and of unwanted children that she had placed by adoption into loving homes. No one spoke. No one needed to. Love had said it all.

Maybe you have been rejected. Perhaps you feel unwanted or uncared for, even today. There is good news. There is One who wants you—and is willing to take you in by adoption as a son or a daughter. His name is Jesus. His love bears all things, believes all things, hopes all things, and endures all things. His love never fails.

## *Prayer of Love*

*Oh Heavenly Father, I exalt the name of Yahweh Rapha, the Lord who heals us. I acknowledge all the hurts and broken relationships that bring me pain.*

*Now I pray to you, O Holy God who is love, teach me to love. Build in me a tough, true, prevailing love for others that is based not on my changing emotions, but on Your changeless nature. Help me to love those whom I would not naturally love, especially those who have hurt me in the past. Help me to understand the height, depth, breadth, and width of Your love for me, and to let that same love flow through me and into others. Love them through me, Lord.*

*Father, I confess that there are those I do not want to love. Change my heart, O God. Refine it with Your fire until it is pure and true. Give me Your eyes to see the needs of others and to understand their fears and weaknesses. Paul said he did not care whether he was loved or not—he was willing to be poured out like a drink offering so that others might come to know You. Oh, that I would have that same reckless abandonment to self and surrender to You.*

*More than anything, God, help me to love You above all else. That is the devotion You demand and the honor You deserve. There is none like You. Shed Your love abroad in my heart by Your Holy Spirit and set it on fire for You. Amen.*

# O Man of God
## The Penny of Hope

*He may not explain to you a thousand things*
*which puzzle your reason in His dealings with you.*
*But if you absolutely sell yourself to be His slave,*
*He will wrap you up in a jealous love, and bestow*
*upon you*
*many blessings which come only to those*
*who are in the inner circle.*
—G. D. Watson

In the years between 1987 and 1991, Rick Amato Ministries was riding a rocket. We began smuggling Bibles into the former Soviet Union just a few months before the winds of history caught us up and launched us out. We put up the sails, and God supplied the power of the wind—just as He always does. By 1991 we had an operating budget of nearly $1.4 million and were quickly approaching our millionth Bible printed in Russia. We had conducted crusades in the Kremlin as well as in several other foreign locales. We'd spoken in Russian schools and facilitated trips into Russia for over five hundred American believers. The energy was incredible—and the results were above and beyond anyone's wildest expectations.

Besides our trips to Russia, Romania, Hungary, and Germany, we sponsored crusades in Brazil, Chile, and Argentina. I had received over four hundred requests to preach at meetings and revivals here in the United States as well. Not only was I doing the work of an evangelist, I was acting as the business manager for Rick Amato Ministries too—an amazing turn of events for a young man who had been on welfare himself just a few short years before.

In 1991 we launched a television ministry, purchasing over a quarter of a million dollars worth of equipment and national air time. I had a deep desire to establish a credible and ethical presence in television evangelism, and we undertook the task with a commitment that we would never solicit a dime from viewers to do it.

While all these incredible things were happening in our ministry, something else was going on in the interior regions of my life. The ministry was exploding, and I was imploding as I began to feel a real loss of power and balance. I had become addicted to work. Kingdom work, yes, but work as a drug—as a way to cover over the areas of my addictive personality that I had yet to deal with completely.

When Jesus saved me from drugs as a teenager, I immediately turned to "religious" activity and became addicted to that. Each time I experienced a crisis in my life, I turned to God, but instead of allowing Him to heal the root of my pain, I simply switched addictions. And I had become quite good at it.

This time, I had developed what is called an *applauded addiction*. No one encourages a drug addict to keep using drugs, but the world urges a workaholic (especially one who's working for God) to keep on going no matter what it costs. It takes tremendous insight and courage to say to someone who is winning people to Christ and proclaiming His word, "Hey, pal—you're an addict." Applauded addictions look good on the outside. People don't try to intervene; they applaud and cheer the addict on. But no matter what kind of good may result, workaholism is compulsive behavior. It has negative consequences on a person's physical and emotional life, as I would soon learn.

## A Prescription for Trouble

In the midst of this whirlwind of activity, I was sleeping only three or four hours a night. I worked nonstop. Before long I began experiencing migraine headaches—a physical manifestation of the stress I was subjecting myself to. (Some people attributed them to the cellular telephone I seemed to have constantly at my ear!) In any case, I took my complaint to a friendly local physician. He ordered an MRI and X-rays, and after viewing them, he assured me that the pain was indeed stress-related. He prescribed medication to alleviate my symptoms—Vicodan for the pain and Soma for muscle relaxation.

I took the drugs as prescribed for nearly three months. I used them separately, exactly as the doctor directed. Gradually, I began to take them together. Then I began to double the dosage, remembering an old maxim: If one feels good, then two or three will feel even better. Before I realized what was happening, I was hooked. Not on illegal drugs this time, but on prescription medicine.

For many years I saw my life as a series of blessings and failures. Now in retrospect, I see it as a cycle of addictions. My addiction to illegal drugs as a teenager became an addiction to religion. My addiction to religion became an addiction to performance for God—to workaholism. My workaholism became an addiction to prescription narcotics. There were no demons tempting me. My life was not totally unmanageable, and, with Jesus Christ in me, I was far from powerless. But addiction occurred—recurred—in my life because of the ways I had learned early on to cope with pain.

## A Wake-up Call

In August of 1991, a friend of mine named Phil Gandy brought me face to face with my problem. Nancy and I and the kids were enjoying a brief—and much needed— holiday in North Carolina. But I was still performing. Only this time, I was doing what I thought good fathers did. I was praying with my kids, spending time with them, loving them, and providing for them. I was faithful to Nancy in my thoughts and conduct. And I was doing the things a good preacher of the gospel does—except for one little problem: I could not stop taking those drugs.

Phil Gandy called me into his bedroom during that trip to North Carolina. His face was grave as he confronted me with these words: "Rick, I want to tell you something. The Spirit of God spoke to me this morning and told me to tell you this: You are taking prescription drugs, and you are addicted to them. If you don't stop right now, God is going to take your life. Rick, are you listening? I said if you don't stop, He is going to take your life!"

I was stunned. My mouth fell open. I tried to keep my voice in control as I answered. "Well, Phil, you are right. I do have a problem. But I don't believe it's as serious as you say. And if God is really going to take my life, I'm going to have to hear it from Him before I'll quit."

Denial. It's one of the strongest forces on the face of the earth. A person in denial knows he has a problem but refuses to assume responsibility for it. Denial is dangerous because 95 percent of it is completely unconscious. There are potholes or cliffs in front of him that others see, but the person in denial does not want to see them for himself. He is angry and defensive, but if you were to confront him with his anger, he would not be aware of it. When an addiction is threatened, it means the addict might have to deal with the root of his pain. In a very real sense, he believes dying would be easier.

When Phil confronted me, God was tenderly trying to lead me into some dark inner places I desperately needed to go. Honesty is the gateway to recovery, and that day there was just a tiny glimmer of honesty in my heart—no more. I did admit to Phil that I was addicted to prescription narcotics, and that was a beginning—however small.

Nancy, the children, and I continued on toward the beach in North Carolina. There we experienced the worst vacation we have ever had as a family. All I could think of now was my addiction. I told myself I had been snared by Satan—again. And in the midst of my dejectedness, I was taking more and more narcotics to find relief and release from the stress I felt. Even in this darkness, God was moving in my heart and trying to help me. It seemed that every verse I read in my Bible talked about judgment for unconfessed and unforsaken sin. Every passage of Scripture seemed to shout of the holiness of God and of His righteousness.

## Quitting Cold Turkey

On the way home from our trip, we stopped at the home of Bradley Brenton, the friend whose condo we had been staying in. Bradley and his wife, Linda, are both physicians and had become great friends to Nancy and me. I realized I was in trouble, but I needed another prescription for the painkillers. I was through lying, though. I told him the truth: "Look, I'm an addict," I said. "I need for you to write me a prescription." He shook his head.

"Rick, I'm sorry," he said. "But I can't give you a prescription. I love you and believe in you, and this is a more common problem than you might believe."

There's not a lot of pride left in a man who begs for drugs from a friend. I made up my mind then and there that I was going to renounce my addiction. I threw what pills I had left out the window, as I had done many times before, and said "I'm finished with this!" Once I had quit illegal drugs cold turkey. I had done it before. I could do it again. But notice the "I" wedged into my resolve: I had always done it all on my own, without any help from anyone else. I had been willing to be honest but not to be broken. I was about to discover brokenness.

The next four months were the loneliest, most bone-chilling days of my entire life. There were many nights that I did not sleep a wink. I developed a neuropathy which continues even now—a feeling like millions of needles penetrating the skin all over my body. Sometimes it felt as if bugs were crawling on my skin. Other times it seemed like hot or cold water was falling on me in sudden, startling splashes. I began to experience frightening hallucinations.

I was forced to cancel all of the meetings I had scheduled during this period. Needless to say, our ministry suffered a severe financial crisis. During the final months of that year, I was suffering unbelievably. I told no one, with the exception of a few close friends whose prayers I desperately needed. For hours and days on end, I wept. I lost my appetite for food. I had no sexual desire. My life became a shipwreck, and my family suffered with me. My children were terrified of me. My wife was struggling to maintain our family's well-being. I was convinced that I would die any day, and I became obsessed with thoughts of death.

## Another Brush with Death

During this time, I discovered that my persistent drug abuse had inflamed my liver. A routine blood test revealed elevated liver enzymes, so my blood was being tested every two or three weeks. One day the telephone rang at my office. It was Nancy.

"The doctor wants you to call him at home," she said. *Why would the doctor give us his home phone number?* I wondered. Thinking the message was very strange, I hung up with her and dialed his number. The message was indeed urgent. My most recent blood test was indicating liver failure. "Rick," he said, "I want you to go straight to the hospital. Now."

"Am I going to die?" I asked.

"It's possible. This is certainly life-threatening," he answered.

I was admitted to the hospital and soon found myself alone with my Bible and a potential death sentence. Frightened and more desperate than ever, I began to search my soul. Although I had a tremendous amount of self-pity, God began to show me that the real victims of substance abuse are not addicts themselves because, in a way, they benefit from their addiction. They escape their pain. As I lay in what I wholeheartedly believed to be my deathbed, I came to understand that the real victims of drug abuse and addiction are the dysfunctional families they cause. Families like the one I had come from and like mine was quickly becoming.

If you've been breathing lately, you've heard the word *dysfunctional*. It comes from two words: *dys,* meaning "wrong," and *functional,* meaning "the way something works." An addict's family simply works the wrong way. Now every family has its problems—don't misunderstand. But if you want to see a truly dysfunctional family, find an addict and follow him home. An addict's family is forced to live with someone whose addiction has become the most important thing in his world. The user wants to use. His family wants him to stop. The family pulls in opposite directions and the "blame game" begins—someone else or something else is tagged as the cause of the trouble.

Once the addict is excused by blaming his problems on something else, maintaining the status quo becomes the order of the day. Everyone must be an enabler, ready with the cover up when it's needed; and someone must assume responsibility for what is wrong. Hence the three golden rules in a dysfunctional family: Don't talk. Don't trust. Don't feel.

During those hours in the hospital, the Spirit of God spoke to me. "Well, Rick," He said, "you've tried to save three hundred million Russians. And you've tried to save half of America and part of South America. Now who is going to save your wife? Who is going to save Beth, your oldest daughter? Who is going to try to save Nancy, her sister? Who is going to save Joseph, your only son? Who will save your twin daughters, Mary and Sara?"

My heart was broken when I realized that no one had ever given me more love and support and affection than my family. Unrelenting waves of shame and remorse washed over me. I had no one to blame but myself. As I lay there struggling with these emotions, the questions began to come: "Who is going to break this cycle? Who will break the curse if I can't? What if it's too late? What if I die before I can make things right?" I began crying out to God in the midst of my confusion and pain: "Oh, God, please—please, God, give me one more chance." Even as I said the words, I knew I must be crazy to ask. God had given me chance after chance after chance, and now I was asking for one more. "Lord Jesus," I breathed, "have mercy on me. Have mercy on me."

For the first time in a long time, I allowed myself to feel my pain. Then as if in response to it, a rush of anger came. I was suddenly infuriated. No one had come to see me yet! No one had even given me a shot since my arrival. The truth was, I wasn't experiencing any physical pain— but I reasoned that if I was going to die this time, I didn't want to be aware of what was happening to me. I wanted morphine—and I got out of my bed and marched down to the nurses' station to ask for a shot.

The nurse at the desk looked up as I approached. "Aren't you Rick Amato?" she asked.

"Yes, I am. Why?"

"Your doctor is on the phone, Mr. Amato. He'd like to speak with you."

She handed me the receiver and I heard the voice of the physician who had admitted me.

"Mr. Amato?" the doctor said, "I just spoke with the laboratory. They have repeated your blood tests, and the diagnosis I gave you earlier was incorrect. In fact, you can go home now."

Those initial test results may have been incorrect—but my hearing them was not a mistake. I realized at that moment that I did not need morphine—I needed deliverance. And real deliverance was something I had yet to experience. I had gotten a temporary reprieve, but healing was still eluding me. I was battered but not broken. That was yet to come.

## Reaching for the Bottom

For the next several months, I continued to struggle on my own to beat my addiction. I never even took so much as an aspirin. I kept myself clean for as long as I could and resumed my preaching—and with it, my very hectic schedule. By December, I was using prescription drugs again. I went back to the same doctor, and he prescribed the same medication. Soon I was taking double and triple doses, just as I'd done before. My work load increased, and I was doing sixteen- to eighteen-hour days, drinking ten cups of coffee or more each morning to get going, and taking pain pills and muscle relaxers to come down at night.

Another wise friend confronted me in February. Larry Claypool came to me and said, "Rick, you don't look right. Are you taking drugs?"

"Yes," I told Larry. "I'm taking prescription drugs again."

At that point he said something that caused my anger, shame, inadequacy, and pain to rise to the surface and spill over. "Rick," he said, "if you don't get help..." (with emphasis on the last two words, *get help*), "if you don't get help, I will never have anything to do with you again."

I'm not sure I realized before that moment that if I did not get help, I was going to die. Larry made it clear. What he also made clear was that I could not stop taking drugs by myself. Our confrontation was the beginning of my journey toward genuine spiritual recovery through the great healer, Jesus Christ. I came to realize that it is possible to know God and still struggle with addiction. Although I knew God and felt assurance of His presence in my life, I had never come to the place where I acknowledged my powerlessness in an area I steadfastly refused to give over to Him.

C. S. Lewis wisely said that to deny God access to any part of our lives is to place ourselves in peril. "When we try to keep within us an area that is our own," he wrote, "we try to keep an area of death. Therefore, in love, He claims all. There is no bargaining with Him." I was only beginning to learn the truth of it.

I put out a call for help. I called a man who had been a paid consultant within the evangelical Christian community for over forty years. "Dr. Neteland," I said, "I need help. I need help now." He cleared his calendar and flew from Los Angeles to Chicago, where arrangements were made for me to be admitted to Edwards Hospital, a medical treatment facility located near Minirith-Meier Clinic. The strategy was for me to undergo detoxification at Edwards, then check into Minirith-Meier for therapy. I had learned from my previous "cold turkey" experience that there was no way my mind or body could tolerate another four months of solo withdrawal.

The doctors at Edwards put me through a comprehensive battery of tests. Their advice was sobering, to say the least: "You can get detoxed here and go home," they said. "Or you can continue as you are, and in two years you will be a dead man." The medical team began morphine detoxification, a procedure which takes four to five days. While they were doing this, Dr. Neteland was working with the hospital business office to determine whether my insurance company would cover the additional treatment recommended at Minirith-Meier.

Meanwhile, I began to experience doubts about the course of action we had agreed to. The old, deceptive thoughts began to creep in again: I can do this on my own. I don't need anybody's help. I've quit drugs many times before, and I can do it again. I argued with the doctors who rightly pleaded for me to stay where I was. The drugs were coming out of my system, but I was far from clean. I was haunted, not by fears of death now but by fears about the disgrace I would bear when my problem became known by more than a handful of close associates. Ironically, the same morning I finally surrendered to the fact that I definitely needed therapy to deal with my addictive personality disorder, a woman from the hospital business office came by to inform me that my insurance would not cover that treatment at Minirith-Meier.

## A Hard Landing

I immediately picked up the phone and called every other treatment center I could think of. I called Narcotics Anonymous and Alcoholics Anonymous; I called my insurance company several times. I called every hotline and helpline in Detroit. The answer was always the same: "We have a long list of people who are trying to get into hospitals for free treatment. Our streets are full of addicts just like you who want help but can't afford it." The words stung me. "Addicts just like you." I was a preacher of the gospel, but I was also just another addict. There were thousands of heroin and cocaine addicts in the streets who had never been to a church and never found Jesus Christ. I had met Him, and yet I was in the same kind of trouble they were. And none of us was getting the help we so desperately needed.

That evening, a hospital attendant arrived in my room with a wheelchair, explaining that I was being discharged.

"Wait a minute," I protested. "You can't check me out yet! I haven't found anyplace to go when I leave here."

"I'm sorry," he said, "but the doctor signed your release today. You'll have to go."

It seemed that up until that day, the medical staff had been begging me to stay—and now they were showing me the door. The doctor gave me one morphine tablet and wrote a prescription for another drug. With that, I was out on the street. Dr. Neteland went to get the car from the hospital parking lot, and I stood on the curb in the middle of Chicago, frightened and freezing to death. I will never forget that moment for the rest of my days. I am thankful now that I did not know what was just ahead.

## The First Step: I Can't

Dr. Neteland checked me into the hotel where he had been staying. I took my last morphine pill at around 6:00 P.M. and went to sleep. In the middle of the night, I woke to what was undoubtedly the worst experience of my life. My body felt as if it were coming apart at the seams. After being on morphine for four days and coming off the other chemicals in my system, my body was crying out for relief. I literally wanted to jump out of my skin.

I called Dr. Neteland's room at 3:00 A.M. in desperation. "Please help me," I cried. "I think I'm going to die." He came into the room and found me on the edge of the bed, shaking and shivering, wishing for death. He simply held me in his arms and rocked me as if I were a little child, reciting to me the words of Psalm 23:

> The LORD is my shepherd, I shall not want. He
> makes me lie down in green pastures; He leads me
> beside quiet waters. He restores my soul; He guides

*me in the paths of righteousness For His name's
sake. Even though I walk through the valley of the
shadow of death, I fear no evil; for Thou art with me;
Thy rod and Thy staff, they comfort me. Thou dost
prepare a table before me in the presence of my
enemies; Thou hast anointed my head with oil; My
cup overflows. Surely goodness and lovingkindness
will follow me all the days of my life, And I will dwell
in the house of the LORD forever (NASB).*

As he prayed for me, my pain grew worse. As powerful a man as he is, there was one thing Dr. Neteland
could not do for me. He couldn't say the words of surrender I needed to say. After he left my room, I took what I
know now was my first step to victory. I had already
acknowledged that if I did not stop using drugs I would
die, and that was true, but it was not enough. I finally
reached the point of total brokenness where I said, "I can't
stop."

Wouldn't it be terrific if we didn't have to reach
bottom to come to a point of surrender to God? But
brokenness in His hands is a penny, and the blessing on
its other side is hope. God's Word confirms that, far from
being disappointed, He is actually pleased when we
come to the end of ourselves, as the psalmist reveals: *"For
Thou dost not delight in sacrifice, otherwise I would give it;
Thou art not pleased with burnt offering. The sacrifices of God
are a broken spirit; A broken and a contrite heart, O God, Thou
wilt not despise"* (Ps. 51:16-17, NASB).

The prophet Isaiah echoes this incredible truth:

*Thus says the Lord, "Heaven is My throne, and
the earth is My footstool. Where then is a house you
could build for Me? And where is a place that I may
rest? For My hand made all these things, thus all
these things came into being," declares the LORD.
"But to this one I will look, To him who is humble*

*and contrite of spirit, and who trembles at My word" (Isa. 66:1-2, NASB).*

As amazing as it may seem, saying "I can't" actually gave me hope. Almost as soon as the words left my mouth, a small voice inside my heart urged me to place a call to Dr. Fred Wolfe. Dr. Wolfe is among the current leaders of the Southern Baptist Convention and is the pastor of the largest church in the state of Alabama. He is a renowned minister of Christ and, thankfully, a dear personal friend as well. I dialed his number, and when I heard his voice, I said, "Dr. Wolfe, this is Rick Amato. I have a serious problem..." Then I related the whole story to him and discovered once again that the One who goes before me had done so this time too.

Even though the hour was quite early and the news I brought him was not good, Fred Wolfe responded to my call with joy in his heart. "You're in luck, Rick," he said. "My son Mark is the director of the Rapha operation in Atlanta—and Rapha is one of the finest Christian psychiatric units in the world. Stay where you are—I'll call you right back."

In the middle of my darkest hour, when I came to the end of myself and realized my brokenness, God gave me hope. And not a false hope—but a hope born out of trial and rightly placed: square on the shoulders of the person of Jesus Christ. The apostle Paul expressed it perfectly in his letter to the Romans:

> *We also exult in our tribulations, knowing that tribulation brings about perseverance; and perseverance, proven character; and proven character, hope; and hope does not disappoint, because the love of God has been poured out within our hearts through the Holy Spirit who was given to us (Rom. 5:3-5, NASB).*

Dr. Wolfe was as good as his word. He called me back in a half hour and said, "Today is your lucky day, Rick.

It just so happens that there is a scholarship bed in the clinic, paid for by generous people. Believe it or not, it's opening up tomorrow. Can you be in Atlanta by 1:30 tomorrow afternoon?"

"Dr. Wolfe," I said, "no matter what it takes, I'll be there. And I don't know how to thank you."

God provided me with a plane ticket through a generous friend, and I arrived in Atlanta, Georgia the next morning, on my way to Rapha. I'm not sure what I expected, but I certainly was not prepared for what I would encounter there. Initially, I was thankful to have found some relief—as they continued my detox process—from the physical pain I was experiencing. But it didn't take me long, as usual, to have second thoughts about being admitted to a psychiatric hospital. What would my friends think? What would happen to the ministry? What would my family do in my absence? How would they feel about my situation? Would they be ashamed of me?

Reality set in when the attendants at Rapha took away my electric razor and my mouthwash (most of which contains a small amount of alcohol). Then the doors shut behind them, and I noticed for the first time that there were no handles on the inside. I was thirty-three years old and literally locked up in a psychiatric ward. I could hardly imagine a worse disgrace.

## The Second Step: God Can

As an abuser of prescription drugs, I had taken step one toward shaking my addiction: I can't. Now I had to take step two: God can. That night, I was asked to attend a group meeting. A group of people were sitting in a circle, and all had been at Rapha longer than I had. I was feeling a little drowsy from the detox medications, but it was easy to see that they were hurting. Many cried, and several talked about an alarming collection of childhood and adult tragedies—from sexual abuse to abandonment to divorce, betrayal, and neglect.

I remember thinking how ridiculous it was that all these people were blaming their addictive behaviors on ancient history. Ann Jones, the therapist who was leading the group seemed to read my mind, and turning to me, she said, "Something is wrong with you too, Rick. Something happened in your past too. You'll see."

"Lady," I said, "I am an addict because I'm a sinner—and that's all there is to it."

Another woman intervened and tried to explain to me that there was more to it than that—that there had to be something that had caused my life to become so unmanageable. I dismissed her.

"Would you be willing to let God show you if we prayed about it?" she asked. A hard request for a minister to refuse. "Sure," I said, in a rather offhand way. "I like to pray." She prayed these words for me: "Lord, I don't know what is in my own heart. But You do. So I ask You to show me—to shine Your light into my heart. Lord, take away from it anything that is wrong or displeasing to You. And show me anything You think I ought to see."

Within minutes, a memory emerged that had been totally hidden from my consciousness before that prayer. It had always been there, of course. It happened to me, so I knew it—I just never treated it as reality and allowed myself to examine it. I saw myself as a young boy, dressed in a pair of blue jeans and a little red shirt, being led into a house on the street where we lived. The house was near the corner and had a big rock in front of it. I saw myself being led down to the basement, and inside, the tools that surrounded the workbench the man placed me on when he sexually abused me.

I almost hesitate to write this because so much is said today about childhood sexual abuse and so many things are blamed on its occurrence. Many are even wrongfully accused of abuse, and the impact of those accusations is devastating. I hated to "cop out" on my own behavior and told the therapist so. "I assume full responsibility for my sin—for my addictive personality," I said. "There are no excuses. I am an addict. Period."

But this painful memory showed me that my addiction had become a way of dealing with my old hurt and shame—and I needed to see that. All of my life I had been trying to win the approval of others, believing that if some significant person would love me, I would be able to feel good about myself. I'd been trying to perform good works to convince myself that I was a good person. I had it all wrong. No earthly love or approval ever satisfies our longing. And no anesthetic ever deadens it. Only Jesus—with the nails in His hands and feet and the wounds in His side—can provide the kind of unconditional love we so desperately crave. Once again, I was led back to the cross.

My response to this awareness was not an appropriate one. Although I thought I was surrendering, what I was really saying was *I can't, but God can. So now I'm going to show Him how.* I refused to take the drugs the doctors gave me to ween me off the pain-killers. A new ambitious pride swelled inside me. I said, "I'm going to quit drugs—right now, on my own."

The nurses and doctors were frustrated and angry with me. Because of my misunderstanding of surrender, I had refused to see the truth they were telling me: I would have to take drugs to quit drugs. Finally I was called in for my five-day review at Rapha. Dr. Michael Lyles, a fine Christian physician from Detroit, said, "Rick, we are going to send you on home."

"Why?" I asked. "I'm just getting started here. I'm just beginning to see 'I can't' and 'God can.'"

Dr. Lyles shook his head. "No, you're not seeing 'God can,' because you won't take the drugs we gave to detox you."

I snapped at him self-righteously. "Listen, Mister! I didn't come here to take drugs, I came here to quit drugs, and you're not going to make me take more drugs."

Dr. Lyles looked me straight in the eyes and said, "This is not about drugs; this is about your surrender. This is about submission to authority. This is about submitting to a higher power."

"I'm submitting to a higher power!" I protested. "I am submitted to God."

"No, you are not." said Dr. Lyles. "If you were submitted to God, you wouldn't be sitting in this psychiatric hospital with a drug problem. The only way you can submit to God right now is to listen to us. We know what is best for you. We've been down this road before."

Then I understood that surrender is not just saying "I can't"—but saying "God can—and I will allow Him to do it any way He chooses." God had chosen to use Rapha and the care available there to restore my broken spirit. And so, with tears in my eyes, I said to the therapists, "Okay, I'll do it your way. I'll take the medicine you prescribe, follow the course of action you outline, and do whatever you want me to do."

To my surprise, this involved resigning my ministry during ninety days of intensive outpatient therapy and being separated from my family during that time. I would spend the next three months attending support groups and undergoing rigorous personal therapy. "I can't" was the first step. "God can" was the second. The final step in my healing process was a sort of continual surrender, deciding every day that I would let Him do what I now knew only He could.

Surrender means saying "I can't, but God can, so I'll let Him."

Surrender means letting go of the past, forgetting the future, and seizing today.

Surrender means getting still and getting close to Jesus.

During my season of brokenness, God moved in my life as He has never moved before or since. Some of the truest words I received during that time were part of a letter given to me by my daughter, Nancy Jean. In it, she quoted the beautiful, familiar passage from Isaiah 40 to her struggling Dad:

> *Hast thou not known? Hast thou not heard that the everlasting God the lord, the Creator of the ends of the earth, fainteth not, neither is weary: there is no searching of his understand. He givith power to the faith: and to them that have no might he increaseth strength. Even the youths shall faint and be weary, and the young men shall utterly fail: But they that wait upon the Lord shall renew their strength: They shall mount up with wings as eagles: they shall run, and not be weary: and they shall walk, and not faint.* (Isaiah 40:28-31, KJV)

It was only when I became faint and had no might of my own that I began to wait on my God. It was then that I came face to face with His sustaining, enabling, ministering power.

The words "faint" and "no might" as used by Isaiah are very suggestive. The idea of "faint" is a weariness from toil, a fatigue brought on by the battle. "No might" means one's creative process or product has been depleted. This described the situation and my feelings precisely.

The word picture is apparent. To those who experience weariness in the battle, to those who say, "I can't go on," God says "if you look you will find a God who is waiting," a God who says, "you can't, but I can!" It is only when we come to the end of ourselves that we will find God waiting to glorify Himself through the broken vessel we have become.

## Facing the Darkside

I knew all about physical healing. I knew I desperately need healing of my soul. I knew about God healing through Narcotics Anonymous and Alcoholics

Anonymous and therapy, but I had always believed that these were "worldly solutions." Like I told everybody when I was younger, "I just like to get high." I thought my problem was simple and all I had to do was stop.

Now, for the first time, I realized that I couldn't stop. My only hope was God and I was about to discover that when we say, "I can't, but God can," we ultimately end up saying, "so I'll let him." "*So I'll let him" anyway He chooses.*

The irony of the process that led to my deliverance is that I was willing to trust Him to save me from sin's penalty, but I was not willing to trust Him to save me from sin's power. In facing the dark side I sought to become His counselor, His advisor. His way was perfect until it clashed with my will. To come completely to the end of oneself is to say, in a renouncing of one's will, "I *can't, God can, so I'll let Him—any way He chooses.*"

He chose to promptly send me to a therapist recommended by Rapha who ordered me to attend ninety meetings of Narcotics Anonymous and Alcoholics Anonymous in ninety days. Thus began my journey on the road to facing the dark side.

I learned more about myself than at any other time in my life. For twenty years I had sought to know God and now He was telling me "know yourself." At this time I learned that addiction is more than drugs and alcohol, cigarettes or being compulsive about sex. I learned that addiction is developmentally acquired system of behaviors learned from the earliest ages of our lives.

When a normal person experiences pain they find the source of the pain and change their lives or circumstances to eliminate the pain. However, an addictive personality is formed when we are either unwilling or unable to face our pain and we instead anesthetize our pain. Some people pour drugs and alcohol on the sting of rejection and bitterness. Others turn to materialism or promiscuous relationships. No matter the drug of choice, the most horrible thing about them is *they work*: at least for awhile.

Eventually, however, the addict not only has the original source of pain, but soon it takes more and more of the anesthetic to kill the original pain until the anesthetic itself becomes an additional and often much more horrible source of pain.

Since that time I now know that I never really dealt with my addictive personality, caused, I believe, by the abuses of my childhood. Now I am not only able to speak freely about them, but I can rejoice in them. I now know what Paul meant when he said, "Most gladly therefore will I rather glory in my infirmities, that the power of Christ may rest upon me." (2Cor. 12:9, KJV)

I no longer see my life as a series of ups and downs, but a cycle of addictions. I now understand that for the longest time after I quit drugs I was a religious addict. Though I was not using drugs or alcohol, my idea of faith was strict conformity to the cultural preferences and rules and regulations set forth by whichever sect of protestantism and its leader/father figure I happened to be with at that time. I desperately needed a father figure to protect me and heal me and take away the pain and trauma of my life. Often I was a pathetic religious slave.

It was during this time of facing the dark side that I learned the difference between being a religious addict and a spiritual Christian. One author notes the difference in this way:

> *Christian life may be nothing more than the acceptance of certain ideas and principles and the observance of certain forms and rites. Christ life is a vital and divine experience through the union of the soul with the living Christ Himself. Christian life may be an honest attempt to imitate Christ and follow His teachings and commandments, but Christ life is the incarnation of Jesus Himself in*

*you own life. It is the Christ reliving His life in you and enabling you to be and to do what, in your own strength, you never could accomplish.*[1]

The difference in a religious addict and a spiritual Christian is simple. The religious addict is marked by a compulsive need to control people. A spiritual Christian is marked by a compulsive need to love people. The religious addict is controlled by the flesh. The spiritual Christian is controlled by the Holy Spirit and thus lives the Christ life. The flesh grabs and consumes, the Spirit gives and cultivates. A religious addict consumes both himself and those around him. A spiritual Christian cultivates both himself and those around him. The difference is dramatic.

This begins with a love for yourself. I'd been taught not to love myself but to deny myself. I was told to love Jesus first, put others second and myself last. When I faced the darkside in my life I finally understood Jesus' words when he said "love your neighbor as yourself." It was then I understood that I really couldn't love anybody else because of all the guilt and shame that I felt towards myself due to my dark side.

When I finally faced the dark side of my soul I was driven once again to Jesus and His Cross where the God of Israel promptly set me free. For the first time ever I realized what I had preached to so many millions. Because of the Cross I no longer had to carry the shame and guilt of my past. I realized that I was deeply loved, totally forgiven, completely accepted and fully pleasing to God. I no longer had to say yes when I wanted to say no. I no longer need the approval of a religious father figure or any other, nor did I need to meet certain standards in order to feel good about myself. Jesus had given me the Heavenly Father's approval and Calvary's performance covered it all.

I needed to cease to focus on being "super preacher," "super husband" and "super dad," but instead on

Rick Amato, the addict, because that was the dark side of my life. It was during this time that a new startling discovery came to me—*the seed to your greatest power is hidden in the heart of your worst problem.*

After I completed my ninety day sojourn into Narcotics Anonymous and Alcoholics Anonymous, I was startled to find much more emphasis on spiritual growth in the healing of the mind there than I had ever found in the church. During those ninety days often I would walk into these Narcotics Anonymous and Alcoholics Anonymous meetings and find that the clientele was a little less than I was used to speaking to in the megachurches of the United States. It wasn't long, though, before I understood that these people were aware of a potent truth—we are not humans having a spiritual experience, we are spiritual creatures having a human experience.

Facing my dark side with these honest, open and willing people caused me to see that the focus of most of the teaching and preaching I had ever heard was about spiritual experiences and the life to come and Heaven with very little emphasis on interpersonal relations and how to deal with the anguish of destructive behaviors toward ourselves or others that we cannot control.

I have spoken with and shared my discovery with so many wonderful Christians who have experienced heartache and heartbreak in their lives due to the controlling influence of religious or other addicts. I am learning that addictive people often are the most controlling people. They must control others outwordly because secretly they themselves are out of control. Children of preachers, doctors, lawyers, have heaped guilt upon themselves and become victims of addictive behavior because of the control factor by well-meaning parents or spiritual leaders who themselves are religious or other types of addicts. Facing the darkside did so much for me. It can do the same for you.

The other amazing thing I learned from Alcoholics Anonymous is that once these people began to tell their stories, it sounded like they were telling mine. Most of them, traumatized as children, learned quickly to escape their pain through addictive behavior and had cycled from addiction to addiction all their lives. Then the most amazing thing happened—I began to change—not just my behaviors either—my thoughts and the secrets of my heart changed.

I know that there is scientific evidence recently issued after a twenty-five year study by the National Institute of Health in Bethesda, Maryland, to prove this. They have demonstrated that when you are traumatized (especially as a child) there are changes within the brain cells. They also proved that there can be healing and further changes in these cells when similarly traumatized victims talk to each other in a small group setting (*American Scientific Journal*, December 1996).

I knew if God was going to heal me it was going to be through other addicts.

We started small groups in my home. Nancy went ballistic about bringing alcoholics and drug addicts to our home. "What about our children? Aren't you afraid of what may happen to them if you bring those people here? This is our home, Rick, our sanctuary. What about keeping our children safe?" But, after much prayer, and because she loves me and wanted so much for me to be healed, she agreed to help form small groups for my sake and the sake of those pilgrims on a similar journey to mine.

So, within a year our group included a lawyer, a microbiologist, a nurse, a certified public accountant, an engineer, a business entrepreneur and a psychotherapist. We discovered that each of us had a dark side we had been dealing with even though we had been in the church for years! None of us had addressed the issues in our lives and we had heaped guilt on ourselves. Years later I now can tell you that many of these people now have ministries of their own, but they minister to people that have the same problem they have. They have found the seed to their greatest power in the heart of their worst problem.

More than that, I now know a deep fellowship with Jesus that I never knew before. I had often wondered why in John, Chapter 13, with his brutal crucifixion on the cross imminent, Jesus began to exult, "Now is the Son of Man glorified, and God is glorified in Him." Strange words for a man about to be butchered. I now understand that had Jesus escaped death, no one would know His name, but because He was crucified, the world's greatest spiritual movement in history bears His name. Because of this Jesus I have allowed God to re-Father me and am discovering that it is from our darkness that His light emerges. Light and darkness are the same to Him, but for us it is only when we look into the darkest corner of our souls, in the place of our most horrible pain, we find that is where God Himself has been waiting for us all along.

The Scripture is clear that we are to "be glad to be weak or insulted or mistreated or to have troubles and suffering if it is for Christ." How can it make such a demand upon us? Because "when I am weak, them am I strong" (2 Cor. 12:10 [CEV]. Like the Hebrew Patriarch Joseph, we must see the darkside as meant by God for our good and His greater glory and say, "They meant it for evil, but God meant it for good" (Gen. 50:20). It is only when you finally look into the darkest corner of your soul that you will discover the brightest light of your spirit. The seed to your greatest power is hidden in the heart of your worst problem. How can this be so? How can it be possible that when I am broken, empty and dead that healing, fullness and life is born? This is the mystery of our Lord Jesus Christ.

It is only when I am crucified with Christ I am truly alive in Christ (Mk. 834, Jn. 12:24, Gal. 2:20)

It is only when I am empty that I can be filled with the Holy Spirit (Eph. 5:18)

It is only when I am weak that I can know the power of His resurrection (2 Cor. 12:9, Phil. 3:10)

It is only as I am foolish that the wise can be confounded (1 Cor. 1:27)

It is only as I am counted as nothing that the great will be brought down (1 Cor. 1:28)

It is only as I become a servant that I am most like my Master (Matt. 10:45, 20:26)

Why is the requirement for deliverance so high? When considering that such action flings the gauntlet of truth in the face of the devil and places the believer in a position of complete abandonment and absolute trust. Why? "In order that no flesh should glory in his presence. That, according as it is written, He that glorieth, let him glory in the Lord." (1 Cor. 1:29, 2 Cor. 10:17)

In the five years that followed the beginning of these small groups we have ministered more effectively to more people in more nations than we ever had in all the previous years put together. We have made a radical alteration from ordinary "ministry" to life-changing deliverance. Now each person I see or deal with in my day to day affairs is a soul Jesus wants to set free. For years I have asked the church how we could liberate others until we ourselves were set free. I now understand that as I allow the Holy Spirit to surgically correct my own soul I become a healer for others. I'm a heart doctor and every person I meet is a candidate for surgery. In my life no addict is safe.

Now we are focusing on a ministry for people who have anxiety attacks, divorced people, people who have lost children —a grief ministry, anyone who has experienced enough pain and darkness to make them willing to probe its corners for the light. Many of those we're helping despair to ever see another flicker of brightness. We're trying to give them hope.

## A Prayer for Hope

*O, Father, I elevate and exalt Your name. You said Your name was Yahweh Nissi—the Lord our standard or banner. You promised that when the enemy comes in like a flood, You would lift up a standard. When the enemy comes in and crushes me, lift up the standard of hope. I want to be a man of God. There are so few heroes in this world, but to be a man of God is to be a true hero. The world says to live for self, but Your word says that to save my life—to keep it for myself— is to lose it eternally. I believe Your Word. God, sometimes I feel so broken by the world and by my own sin and selfishness. I don't see how You could possibly use me when I'm defeated and beaten down, but I'm grateful that You do. In fact, those are the times when I feel Your presence more strongly than ever! Father, in my brokenness show me Your hope. Help me to see like the apostle Paul that the end of my defeat is the beginning of Your victory; to exult in my tribulation, knowing that "tribulation brings about perseverance; and perseverance, proven character; and proven character, hope; and hope does not disappoint, because the love of God has been poured out within our hearts through the Holy Spirit who was given to us."*

*Nothing makes me more hopeful than this: knowing that when I was completely without hope, Jesus died for me. While I was nothing but a full-time sinner, He gave Himself for me. God of hope, never let me forget who You are and what You did for me. "My hope is built on nothing less than Jesus' blood and righteousness." Even in my brokenness, I will worship You in His name. Amen.*

# Hope for the Walking Wounded

## The Penny of Perseverance

Someone has said, "What God uses He bruises." I say what He makes He first breaks. If you are serious about being used by God, you will experience periods of brokenness too. A recent survey of pastors by the Fuller Institute of Church Growth reports that 50 percent felt unable to meet the needs of their job, and 75 percent reported a significant, stress-related crisis at some point during their ministry. Dr. James Dobson reports that 40 percent of pastors surveyed by Focus on the Family said they have considered leaving the pastorate in the last three months! It's hard to be a man of God, in or out of the pulpit. Just listen to the suffering experienced by one seasoned veteran in ministry:

> *Five times I received from the Jews thirty-nine lashes. Three times I was beaten with rods, once I was stoned, three times I was shipwrecked, a night and a day I have spent in the deep. I have been on frequent journeys, in dangers from rivers, dangers from robbers, dangers from my countrymen, dangers from the Gentiles, dangers in the city, dangers in the wilderness, dangers on the sea, dangers among false brethren; I have been in labor and hardship, through many sleepless nights, in hunger and thirst, often without food, in cold and exposure. Apart from such external things, there is the daily pressure upon me of concern for all the churches (2 Cor. 11:24-28, NASB).*

Paul knew what it was to be broken. Writing to his young companion Timothy from a Roman prison not long before his death, he asked for him to come and bring *"the cloak which I left at Troas with Carpus, and the books, especially the parchments . . . Make every effort to come before winter"* (2 Tim. 4:13, 21, NASB). At the end of his life, Paul—preacher of the gospel, planter of churches, and defender of the faith—was a lonely, tired, and cold old man, longing for the comfort of a coat and the encouragement of the Word of God.

A few years ago, I was in Rome with my two oldest daughters, Beth and Nancy Jean. They were more interested in shopping than in ruins and museums, but one afternoon they humored their dad and we visited the place where historians now believe the apostle Paul lies buried. I thought of how tiny and dark his dungeon cell must have been, with barely enough space to turn his body over. Of how cold and dank it was—and how he longed to warm himself with a cloak and the precious Word of God. We were there in the month of July, and it was a difficult time for me, personally. But I took courage from tarrying near the final resting place of this man of God.

The girls were sweet about this unscheduled stop, but they're teenagers. "Come on, Daddy, let's go," they pleaded. But I stayed. And I saw him. I saw him raise his once-strong arm and say these words: *I have fought the good fight, I have finished the course, I have kept the faith; in the future there is laid up for me the crown of righteousness, which the Lord, the righteous Judge, will award to me on that day; and not only to me, but also to all who have loved His appearing* (2 Tim. 4:7-8, NASB). And He says it not only to me but to all who have loved His appearing! That's me. That's you. That's us.

Reluctantly, I left, but I returned later in a taxi, as if drawn by a magnet. I had to be there. Again. As I stood and looked once more at the place where his bones were, I remembered that he died a broken man. Known

by many but loved by only a loyal few, often understood by the Master alone, Nero was the most powerful man in the world—and at Nero's hand he suffered
the indignity of a horrible death. He died in shame and
in absolute poverty, seemingly a failure.

Then I realized that nearby stood an edifice worth
billions of dollars, gleaming with gold adornment and
full of the world's richest treasures in art and
artistry—a basilica that bore the name Saint Paul. My
heart filled with unspeakable joy as I felt the presence
of all those saints who walked this path before me,
leaving a map for me and for you to follow—a map of
hope for all mankind, for my children, your children
and their children. I felt so humbled by the fact that the
ground upon which I stood was the very same ground
that Paul had stood upon so long ago. Thousands of
years later, we revere Paul as the man of God that he
was, while Nero is scarcely remembered. Men today
name their dogs Nero, but they name their sons Paul!

Man of God, woman of God—are you broken
today? There is hope. Brokenness is a penny. Hope is a
miracle. And knowing God is all that really matters. I
pray that these pages have given you a fresh glimpse of
the Living God. Yes, He's real. Yes, He loves you and
me, in spite of our addictions, our foolish choices, our
idolatries and our shortcomings. Even when we are
faithless, He is faithful. It's who He is. It's all that He
can be. And the best news I can give you is this: if you
want to know Him, you will find Him. Ask Him to
reveal Himself to you today.

When you do, remember you must abandon every
preconceived notion you have about Him. You must
look away from all the idols of this earth, even the reli-
gions of men. When you say "God reveal yourself to
me," you must begin with the "to me" part. You have
to start with your own dark side. Also, you must realize that when you ask God to reveal Himself to you,
you ask Him to do it any way He chooses.

When you do, you'll be surprised at the coincidences that begin to happen in your life, in the miracles that God will do to make you know His love for you. I call these miracles pennies and today I believe God wants to share them with you. The penny of hope, of promise, is waiting to be discovered by you. Pick it up, hold it in your hand, put it in your pocket. Know God and make Him known. This is the answer to all those children who will walk after us. You and I can make a difference because you and I can be different. Believe that God is lighting you path. Then you too can face the darkest corner in your life and in that darkness you will find a light brighter than the noonday sun. As you walk the path, if you just keep your eyes open, you will see there are pennies scattered everywhere.

I know. I have a pocket full of them.

## A Prayer for Perseverance

*Oh God, You are known as* The Everlasting One *and I revere and hallow that Holy Name.*

*You are outside the confines of time and space and gravity. God You* **are** *eternal.*

*Thank You for the inheritance You have given me that will never perish, spoil or face. I confess You are not only all I want but all there really is.*

*I ask You, in the name of the One who persevered all the way past the Cross to the empty tomb. . . give me strength! Help me transcend my own perception of my limits and show me not how strong I am but how strong You are in me.*

*Give me the grace of perseverance so that even if I may not win the race I will not quit running it. May I run with the endurance that only You can give knowing that Your smiling face is the only prize I seek and finishing was all that You asked.*

*That You let me know You are running beside me is all I ask.*

*In Jesus' name I pray*

# WHO IS RICK AMATO?

Dr. Rick Amato is a cutting-edge evangelist, leading the Christian faith in the new Millennium. The Rick Amato story is about hope. It's about change. It's about finding God's hidden power in the heart of your worst problem.

Rick Amato's story begins in a Detroit suburb where he became a drug addict and alcoholic. After several relapses to drugs and a wild ride that included travel through over 40 nations and almost all 50 states as an itinerate preacher, Amato was finally hospitalized in 1986 in the welfare ward of a local hospital as a prescription drug addict.

That's when Amato realized that when you get to the place where knowing God is all that you have left, you finally discover that knowing God is all there really is.

Since then he founded Rick Amato Ministries (RAM). RAM is committed to knowing God and making Him known around the world. RAM has many different programs that reach into various parts of the ever-changing culture, with the unchanging message of the Cross.

Rick Amato received an honorary Doctorate of Divinity from Liberty University in 2001, and was also named the national and international chaplain of AWANA (one of the world's most respected youth movements) in the same year.

Rick Amato and his wife Nancy, who have been together for over 25 years, reside in Michigan with their five children and grandchildren.

Who is Rick Amato? A simple preacher of the Cross.

# How Can You Be Part of a Significant Work for God?

*Dr. Rick Amato's vision is* **to know God and make Him known** *to others. Here's how you can join him as he lives out this vision. First by . . .*

## 1) KNOWING GOD

*You can know God by joining Rick on his own personal journey with these resources that will minister to your specific needs.*

## <u>*TO GOD E THE GLORY!*</u>

Now you can read a miracle story from Rick and our many RAM Partners each day. Visit <u>www.rickamato.com</u> and click on the Pennies-A-Day story. These miraculous stories will inspire you to know God and to make Him known in your own walk. As you begin to discover the pennies in your own life. You can write your story to be considered for posting on our Pennies-A-Day web page. E-Mail your stories directly from the website.

# <u>Addiction</u>

*This booklet will help you find the power to defeat addiction in the life of yourself or your loved ones. Learn the truth about addiction, find the causes of addiction, and discover the only way to be set free from the awful horrors of addiction. You will never be the same again!*

# Depression

This booklet tells how you or someone you love can deal with depression. These pages will teach how God's light can shine into the darkest situations of your life and give you back the joy and serenity of life you don't have now!

# Panic Attacks

This booklet will help you turn your defeats into triumphs, and your failures into victories. It will open your eyes to the truth that "the seed to your greatest power is hidden in the heart of your worst problem."

Call **1-800-543-WORD** today or visit
_www.rickamato.com_ to order these exciting new
booklets from RAM for only $3.

# 1) KNOWING GOD

*You can make God known by taking part in some of these various ministries of RAM.*

**RICK AMATO MINISTRIES** is a worldwide evangelistic organization that ministers to the people of America through local church meetings, special youth meetings, and citywide crusades. *RAM* has spoken to millions through television and various other venues. *RAM* has recorded hundreds of thousands of decisions in the past twenty years.

**RAMCARE** is the international humanitarian and medical arm of RAM. *RAMCARE* specializes in the post-socialist nations such as Russia, Cuba, China, and India. *RAMCARE* has placed well over a million Scriptures in Russia, and millions of dollars in medicine to Cuba as well as other countries. This outreach needs volunteers who will journey with RAM on these trips.

The **POWER OF CHOICE** campaign is focused to educate and inspire the public school students of America. "The Power of A Choice" is the message to young people about the fact that we have the power to choose be cannot choose the consequences of our choices. FOX'S James Brown, Congressman Steve Largent, and Survivor 2 contestant Mike Skupin, are all supporters of this amazing program which has reached all the way to the President of the United States. The *POWER OF CHOICE* has been personally presented to over 250,000 public school students in recent years.

The **ANTIOCH INITIATIVE** is a partnership between the local church pastor and evangelist Rick Amato. It is a modern-day Acts story of Paul and Barnabas. This groundbreaking program bridges the gap between evangelism and discipleship. Utilizing evangelistic crusades and small group leadership training, local church members are trained in evangelism.

**RAM PARTNERS Message of the Month Club**—RAM Partners Message of the Month Members receive a monthly message prepared especially for them by Dr. Rick Amato from one of his sermons preached in a live event. These up to date messages include many current and prophetic events from the cutting edge of the exciting world of evangelism and discipleship. One person said, *"I live from month to month to receive these messages. I make copies of them and give them to all my loved ones and have seen God work miraculously. My son listened to your pocketful of pennies cassette so much that he wore it out. Never quit sending me these messages."*

**Also by becoming a RAM Partners Message of the Month Club member you will have priority access to resources such as . . .**

**The Last Generation**—A cutting edge video that answers the question millions are asking in the new millennium, "Are we the last generation?" (#72213)

**Quest For The Lost Tribes**—An epic video documentary searching for the truth behind one of the Bible's greatest prophecies of the return of the lost tribes of Israel to Jerusalem. (#72214)

**How To Defeat Addiction**—A powerful video that will help to release you or someone you know from the horrors of addiction. (#72205)

**Operation: Recovery**—A four-tape discussion about the affects and treatment of addiction. (#72204)

**How To Defeat Depression**—A life-changing video that will aid you or a loved one in defeating depression. (#72203)

**Operation: Deliverance**—A four-tape audio series discussing how you or someone you know can be delivered from the grip of depression. (#72202)

**New Horizons To Peace**—A two-tape discussion with panic attack sufferers and a professional psychologist. (#72206)

**Finding God's Hidden Power**—An anointed sermon by Rick Amato available on audio (#72207) and video (#72209) cassette.

**The Power of Prayer**—A powerful sermon by Rick Amato. Learn how the power of prayer can change your life forever! Contains video footage of Rick Amato's rare interview with Mikhail Gorbachev. (#72211)

**Living In the Shadow of Shaddai**—A video that teaches you "that the secret to God's presence is His presona when you are in secret." You'll learn to pray the names of God and live your life in the shadow of the almighty. (#72216)

*Audio and/or Video cassettes are also available that deal with such topics as, the second coming, and evangelism; as well as many other topics. To order these or other various resources, please* **call** 800-543-**WORD** *or visit* **www.rickamato.com**.

## "STONES OF REMEMBRANCE"
### *A new book by Dr. Rick Amato*

*I will always sing about the Lord's love; I will tell of his loyalty from now on. I will say, "Your love continues forever; your loyalty goes on and on like the sky."*
Psalm 89:1–2

In his next book Rick Amato shares how the pennies in your life become "Stones of Remembrance" that remind us of the presence of God in our lives and teach us how to chronicle His work from the past, to take us to new levels in the future.

**Look for the new book "Stones of Remembrance" by Dr. Rick Amato coming from Thomas Nelson, Inc. Spring 2002!**